ORAL LANGUAGE RESOURCE BOOK

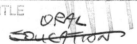

The *Oral Language: Resource Book* was researched, developed and written by Leanne Allen in the context of the Gosnells Oral Language Project. Jennifer Evans assisted with the production of the written material. Caroline Barratt-Pugh, Edith Cowan University, and Anna Sinclair, Education Department of Western Australia, contributed the chapter on Supporting Diversity Through Oral Language.

First Steps was developed by the Education Department of Western Australia under the direction of Alison Dewsbury.

Rigby Heinemann

Rigby Heinemann
a division of Reed International Books Australia Pty Ltd
22 Salmon Street, Port Melbourne, Victoria 3207
World Wide Web http://www.rigby.heinemann.com.au
Email info@rigby.heinemann.com.au

Offices in Sydney, Brisbane, Perth and Adelaide. Associated
companies, branches and representatives throughout the world.

Published by Rigby Heinemann on behalf of the Education
Department of Western Australia

2001 2000 1999 1998 1997
10 9 8 7 6 5 4 3 2 1

Cataloguing-in-publication data

Oral language: resource book

ISBN 0 7312 2360 8

1. Oral communication - Study and teaching (Primary).
2. Language arts (Primary). 1. Western Australia.
Education Dept. (Series: First steps (Perth, W.A.)).

372.622

Contents

General Introduction

The First Steps *Oral Language: Resource Book* complements the *Oral Language: Developmental Continuum* and aims to provide teachers with additional ideas for teaching students about oral language. Many of the ideas suggested can be modified for use with children at different developmental phases.

The *Oral Language: Resource Book* contains detailed descriptions of strategies in the same three main indicator areas as the *Oral Language: Developmental Continuum*, that is Language and Literacy, Language of Social Interaction, and Language and Thinking. Each area has three distinct strategy sections. The Language and Literacy area has strategies for Newstelling, Narrative and Description activities. The Language of Social Interaction area contains strategies for Activity-based Sharing, Discussion and Social Conventions. The Language and Thinking area has strategies for Partner Work, Inquiry and Classification.

Each strategy is introduced in stages and there are many teaching points included. There are also ideas for assessment of children's progress in each area.

The *Oral Language: Resource Book* gives teachers many suggestions for including oral language in all areas of the curriculum.

Oral Language Framework

The Oral Language Framework was designed to reflect three kinds of talk: Language of Social Interaction, Language of Literacy and Language of Thinking.

Each area was further developed to provide opportunities for children to use language for a range of audiences and purposes. Although the areas are outlined in separate chapters, they are interrelated and complement each other. Each recognises that speaking, listening, reading and writing have a role in communication and that development in one area is linked to development in the others.

AREA (Chapter)	SECTIONS
Language of Social Interaction	Activity-based Sharing
	Discussion
	Social Conventions
Language and Literacy	Newstelling
	Narrative
	Description
Language and Thinking	Partner Work
	Inquiry
	Classification

Chapter 1

Language of Social Interaction

- **Activity-based Sharing**
- **Discussion**
- **Social Conventions**

Section 1:

Activity-based Sharing

Speaking and listening are the forms of language most frequently used to explore new knowledge, to understand new experiences and to develop new meanings. In the classroom, learning is stimulated in many ways. For example, children gather new information by observing, listening to others, practising skills, or experimenting with ideas and materials. Knowledge and understanding are consolidated as children use language to classify, organise or reflect upon their experiences.

An effective way to assist children to come to terms with new experiences and create new meanings is through opportunities to share experiences with peers and adults. Meaningful sharing sessions challenge children to express their opinions, to think, to make hypotheses, to speculate, to express doubts, to draw conclusions, to question, to make comparisons, to explain and to listen and respond to others. Through purposeful talking and listening, children can test their understandings and make modifications to their thinking and knowledge.

The activity-based sharing activities outlined in this section encourage children to become active participants in learning through meaningful speaking and listening experiences across the curriculum. Ideas for sharing sessions range from informal activity-based talk to more formal classroom presentations that require a higher level of reflection and planning. They are suitable for partner, small-group or whole-class activities and can be adapted for any age or ability level. All focus on subject-related activities where the teacher can structure content, vocabulary or process.

Activity-based sharing promotes learning through:

- **Speaking and Listening** – *formulating ideas and concepts by talking with adults and peers for real purposes.*

- **Reflection** – *reflecting on what has been accomplished before communicating understandings to others. This may require the child to recall how a task was planned and completed, to identify difficulties or successes, and to evaluate what was learned from the experience.*

- **Classroom Interaction** – *engaging in both formal and informal interactions that place different demands on the way language is used. For example, during group activities, language is spontaneous and children's attention is focused on the task rather than talk itself. In more formal presentations, children are conscious of the way they are speaking and the level of information required by the audience.*

The Language of Activity-based Sharing

Children move through recognisable stages as they develop the language skills necessary for activity-based sharing.

At kindergarten level, sharing is a spontaneous behaviour arising naturally from what children do or observe. Language skills at this stage generally involve labelling or giving simple descriptions that focus on selected attributes of an item, e.g. *This is a truck and it's red*. Teacher support is usually needed to extend language beyond those features that immediately capture the children's attention.
(Note: Throughout this book 'kindergarten' will be used as the term for the year prior to formal schooling which is not compulsory in many parts of the world.)

When children begin primary school there is an enormous growth in knowledge, skills and independence. Classrooms promote learning by providing children with a range of activities and resources that motivate them to explore their environment and share discoveries with teachers and peers. At this stage, children display an increasing ability to incorporate more detailed and systematic information into their descriptions. They also begin to judge and adapt their presentations to suit the needs of the listener.

As children continue through primary school they provide descriptions or explanations that are more sophisticated and abstract. They begin to focus less on the surface features of an item and more on the process involved in producing it. A typical sharing session might include the goal of the task, planning, steps involved, difficulties encountered and their resolution. This ability to stand back and reflect on a task marks a new stage of language development. At this point, children begin to incorporate an evaluative element in their sharing or discussion. They consciously assess the task, comment on both the product and process, and draw parallels with previous activities and experiences.

Activity-based language skills are developed in four stages:

Labelling parts of work ✛	*This is the dinosaur and this is the baby dinosaur.*
Describing work ✛	*This is a green and blue dinosaur and it's got spikes. This boy is scared because the dinosaur is going to eat him.*
Explaining how work was produced ✛	*I drew the big one first. Then I drew this little one hiding behind the rock and I cut out some green paper to do their skin.*
Reflecting on process and product	*I like this one best because it's got lots of colours. I'm going to call it Rainbow Dinosaur. I'm going to draw some more things for it to eat but I haven't decided what yet. My brother's got a dinosaur book at home. I could look up what dinosaurs eat in that.*

Teachers can promote language skills by providing a classroom environment that encourages children to become active participants in the learning process. The following transcripts illustrate the developmental path in activity-based sharing.

Candice (Kindergarten):

That's a stamp. And then you have to colour it in. You have to make some patterns. Oh, you can have different colours. Well, you have to do some stamps. You have to colour it in.

Robert (Year 1):

I did the Five Little Monkeys sheet ... and it was mixed up words ... and they were mixed up and you had to cut them and glue them. And I'll tell you what it says ... And after you glued you had to colour the pictures and I read it to Michael and it was good.

Rory (Year 3):

Well, I did this story map one and that's the one I like the best. I tried really hard and it looks nice ... um ... and it was easy to do, too. This one needed two sheets 'cause you had to colour the things Grandpa Poss and um ... whatsit ... yeah, Hush had to eat and then you had to cut them out and glue them onto this sheet about Australia. And this is a map with the different places where they had the food like, um, Anzac biscuits in Adelaide. Then I jazzed it up a bit by colouring the places in different colours. I tried to make it go all the one way and I think I did a good job.

Activity-based sharing develops both social and language skills. Social skills include:

- increased confidence and participation
- awareness of speaking and listening roles
- understanding of group interaction as a strategy for learning

Language skills develop when children are required to:

- reflect on the task
- select and organise information
- judge the level of explanation required by the audience
- adopt a language style appropriate to the setting and audience

Contexts for Sharing

The choice of context and level of teacher support will determine how quickly children demonstrate independence during sharing time.

Selection of any sharing context should be seen as a tool for moving children from teacher-facilitated sharing to confident and independent use of language.

The following contexts can be incorporated into curriculum areas at all Year levels. It is suggested that teachers provide a balance of both informal and formal activities.

Informal Sharing	Structured Sharing	Independent Sharing	Formal Sharing
• Activity-related talk • Individual child-adult sharing • Informal classroom sharing and discussion	• The sharing circle	• Partner sharing • Small-group sharing	• Rostered whole-class sharing • Inter-class presentations • Assembly presentations • Community involvement

Informal Sharing

Activity-related Talk

Encourage children to share and discuss the activity in progress. Effective interaction at this stage ensures more detailed recall when children share at the conclusion of the activity.

Curriculum Areas:
- mathematics
- art
- social studies
- science
- health

Activity-related talk

Individual Child-Adult Sharing

Organise children to share individual work with a teacher or parent. This is an effective starting point for children who lack confidence in more formal situations. Such children benefit from the opportunity to develop language skills with the support of adult questions and comments.

Curriculum Areas:

- activity mathematics
- art
- social studies
- science
- health
- reading activities

Individual child-adult sharing

Informal Classroom Sharing and Discussion

Introduce informal sharing sessions to review classroom activities or to provide a natural lead-in to the Circle Sharing Strategy. For example, discuss recent classroom experiences and facilitate recall through questioning and commenting. Occasionally, record group discussion by scribing or drawing information.

Curriculum Areas:

- mathematics
- reading
- writing
- art
- social studies
- science

Informal classroom sharing and discussion

Structured Sharing

Sharing Circle

Implement this strategy as a whole-class or small-group activity. Have children take turns around the circle to present and talk about an item of work and guide sharing through questioning and feedback. In addition, invite class members to respond to, or question, each speaker.

Curriculum Areas:

- reading
- writing
- art
- social studies
- science
- health
- mathematics

Sharing circle

Partner Sharing

Instruct children to share their work with a nominated partner during allocated sharing times, e.g. at the conclusion of problem-solving maths sessions, or during art activities. Alternatively, have children choose a friend with whom to share their work.

Partner sharing is an effective strategy when there is insufficient time for whole-class sharing.

Curriculum Areas:

- mathematics
- science
- social studies
- health
- art

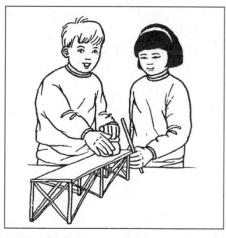

Partner sharing

Small-group Sharing

Introduce small-group sharing with teacher facilitation. When children are familiar with the routine, have them run their own activity-based sharing sessions in groups of three or four. Introduce subject areas through *authors' circle, artists' circle, mathematicians' circle* etc.

Curriculum Areas:

- mathematics
- writing
- art

Small-group sharing

Formal Sharing

Rostered Whole-class Sharing

Roster children on a daily or weekly basis to share their work in front of the class. Since this approach involves planning for a more formal presentation, children should be given a framework for organising the content of their talk (see Content Frameworks, page 15).

Curriculum Areas:

- science
- social studies
- mathematics
- health

Rostered whole-class sharing

8

Inter-class Presentations

Have children prepare an item of interest to show another class. Assist each child to prepare a brief explanation of how and why it was produced. Organise the sharing time as a partner activity or a more formal class presentation.

Curriculum Areas:

- reading
- science
- writing
- social studies
- health
- art

Inter-class presentations

Assemblies

Choose a piece of work to present at assembly and have children prepare a brief explanation for the audience. If possible, encourage children to present the information independently, or provide palm cards to assist planning and presentation.

Assemblies

Community Involvement

Provide opportunities for children to interact with community members through interviewing, collecting activity-based history, drama or public speaking.

Community involvement

Teaching Strategies

Sharing Circle

The Sharing Circle is the main instructional strategy for developing independent sharing skills. The strategy increases children's ability to provide detailed information and descriptions. It also promotes a greater awareness of audience needs as children add or clarify information in response to the listeners' comments or questions.

Procedure:

1 At the conclusion of an activity, instruct the children to choose a piece of work and form a sharing circle.

2 Explain the task; for example:
People have been very busy this week doing different activities. Now we're going to find out about the different things people have been doing. This is our sharing circle. It's where we come to show each other things we've done or made. This way we get to find out about other people's good ideas. When it's your turn to share, I want you to put your work in a place where we can all see it, and tell us about it.

3 Model a presentation using one of the frameworks outlined on page 15.

4 Allow planning time. This can be an individual thinking time or a practice sharing time with a peer.
First prepare what you are going to say. Try to think of all the different things you could tell us.

5 Invite, or select, children to have turns. Support and extend their activity-based sharing with questions and comments. In addition, refer to the charts to assist children in their planning and presentation.

6 Encourage questions and comments from other children in the group.

7 Reinforce aspects of children's sharing to support the current teaching focus; for example:
   • adding more detail to explanations
   • using subject-specific vocabulary
   • sharing interesting ideas and discoveries

The Teacher's Role in Sharing

Sharing makes special demands on speaking and listening. To ensure that children are clear about their role as speakers and listeners, they need to become familiar with the sharing routine. They also need appropriate teacher modelling and questioning to develop the content of each topic.

The long-term goal of sharing is to encourage children to begin sharing confidently and independently with minimal teacher support. When conducting sharing sessions, aim to reduce teacher input as children become more familiar with the procedure. A decreasing dependence on teacher facilitation will lead directly to an increase in peer questioning and the development of effective discussion skills.

Eventually, teacher involvement should consist of participation simply as a group member with occasional intervention when extra facilitation is needed. This shift to a less direct role still plays an important part in promoting independent sharing.

Sharing should have an informal role at pre-primary level. At this stage, many children simply enjoy participating and any attempts to introduce formal instruction may reduce their motivation to share.

If necessary, adapt the Circle Sharing Strategy by placing a hoop in the middle of the sharing circle. Encourage children to focus their attention on each item as it is placed in the hoop. If children are inhibited by the school environment, or if their 'language of home' is different from that of the teacher, model the vocabulary and patterns of language necessary to provide simple descriptions or explanations. When children are familiar with the routine, organise informal or independent sessions at activity or learning centres. Children who wish to participate, or observe, sit around the hoop.

Initially, implement the Circle Story Strategy with groups of three or four children. This approach caters for limited concentration spans. It also provides a safe, supportive setting for children who lack confidence in sharing with a larger group.

Teaching Points

- Identify specific skills needed for activity-based sharing; for example:
  Melissa's remembered a good way of showing her work. She's put it in a spot where everyone can see it.
  You need to think of the best words to describe your item.

- Provide concrete strategies for introducing the item or topic. This is important for children who need to develop independence; for example:
  I like the way Michael started his sharing. Can you remember what he said right at the beginning? He said, 'This is a ...'
  Can you remember how John introduced his explanation?

- Encourage children to sort out ideas independently. Allow some thinking or practice times to reduce the need for teacher support when children begin to share; for example:
  Often it helps to plan what you're going to talk about before you do your sharing. I'm going to give you some time to do some thinking ... OK ... Now have a talk to the person sitting next to you about the ideas you had.

- Be explicit about speaking and listening roles so children can monitor their own performance. Identify special tasks or routines for speakers and listeners to follow. This helps the transition from the sharing circle to independent sharing; for example:
  At the end of your partner sharing, think of one question to ask... tell your partner one thing you like about what he or she's done or the way he/she explained it... share an idea about something he/she could add to the work.

Developing Content

The level of content included in an activity-based sharing session will vary between Year and phase of development. For example, kindergarten children may simply label an item and point out one or two features. Older children may include an introduction, description of special features and the steps involved in creating them. In general, however, all activities should be complex and challenging enough to motivate children to provide sufficient or elaborated information for the listener. Subject-specific vocabulary should be included, particularly if the activity is related to a nominated curriculum area, e.g. mathematics or science. In addition, children should be encouraged to make reflective comments on a completed task. This is possible if a question time is included where children are asked to give their opinions about the outcome of the lesson, e.g. difficulties in planning, working with a partner or completing the task.

When formulating questions, the teacher needs to remain flexible and responsive to the children's lead. Sometimes what children view as important or interesting about an item differs from an adult's interpretation.

The following framework assists teachers to identify a child's stage of content development. It also provides information for generating teaching objectives. Children with highly-developed activity-based language skills will demonstrate most of the following elements in their presentations.

STAGES OF DEVELOPMENT

Stage	Indicators	Teacher Facilitation
Introducing or labelling work	Children: • make general statement about the item being shared • provide outline of goal or purpose of activity • label parts of work	*I used a thick black texta to write the words.* *Oops, I forgot to tell you what I put in the sharing circle. That's the first thing I need to say.* *James introduced his work very well. Can you remember what he said at the beginning?* *He said...I like the way Jenny pointed out all the things in the picture and said what they were.*
Describing work	• describe or explain special features	*I think that part of the ship you're telling us about is called the deck.* *I can see that this car has... Are there any other special things about it? What can it do?* *You've drawn special patterns on your Easter eggs. Tell us about all the different kinds of Easter eggs your Easter bunny has in his basket.* *I enjoyed the way Lisa gave us lots of details about the person she drew. She thought of lots of little things she wanted us to notice about her picture.*
Explaining how work was produced	• list materials • outline steps • explain planning and decision making • describe problems and solutions • include other information, e.g. time taken, help given, unfinished sections	*Your giant looks different from Ryan's. Can you tell us some things about how you made it?* *What things did you use?* *Michael explained really well. If I had to do the worksheet I would know all the steps.* *Why did you draw the giant with an extra eye?* *How did you make it into a purple colour?* *Were there any parts you had to plan first?* *Did you have any problems? How did you work out what to do?*
Reflecting on process and product	• add specific comments about the task, e.g. similarity to a previous task • include comments about what was learned from the task, e.g. how task would be tackled next time	*Have you done anything like this before?* *What is hard?* *Would you do it the same way if you did it again? What would you change? What would you keep the same? What part are you proudest of? Why?* *Where did you get the idea about...? Was that the first idea you thought about? How did you decide?* *If you were explaining to someone who hadn't done something like this before, what is the main thing you would tell them to remember?* *What new things did you learn by doing the activity?* *Where else do you think you could use Sarah's idea about..?*

Developing Vocabulary

The Stages of Development, i.e. *Introducing the item, Describing the item, Explaining how work was produced, Reflecting on process and product*, can be used in three ways:

1 To informally monitor children's development of activity-based sharing skills, i.e. *Can the children describe the item or explain the activity?*

2   As a framework to guide teacher questioning and facilitation.

3   As a framework that is explicitly taught to children.

Activities that involve activity-based sharing sessions enable children to learn vocabulary by hearing and using words in contexts that are meaningful to them. For example, a teacher may introduce the following vocabulary during maths activities: *level, balance, unbalanced, heavier, scales, measure, estimate*. During group activities, children have the opportunity to use and practise these words while interacting with their peers. In preparing for the sharing session they are encouraged to focus on the completed activity and select the most appropriate vocabulary to describe or explain the task to the class. Children who have incorporated mathematical terminology in spontaneous talk will have little difficulty introducing the vocabulary in more formal presentations.

Sharing activities are also effective for children learning English as a second language. For example, the teacher may structure the lesson so that the children are introduced to an activity in English, before completing a group task using their first language. During sharing time the children reflect on the task and attempt to present their information in English. This type of organisation allows children to solve a problem or complete an activity using the language in which they are most competent, while allowing the teacher to monitor the lesson and introduce English vocabulary, where appropriate. It also provides opportunities for children to practise the patterns and structures of English using an immediate experience as a springboard. It is important that children whose 'language of home' is different from that of the teacher are able to code-switch if they feel the need.

When children are having difficulty including sufficient information in an activity-based sharing session, the following frameworks can be introduced to provide support for planning and presentations. This is a more structured approach and one that is probably most appropriate for more formal presentations. During the session, children are presented with a framework to plan and monitor the content of their activity-based presentation. The steps are displayed on charts and the teacher initially models how to plan and present the information. For subject-specific activities, include displays of appropriate vocabulary.

Tell us what you made	Tell us how you made it

• What is it called?	• What did you use to make it?
• What does it look like?	• What were the steps?
• How do you use it?	• What things did you have to remember while you were doing it?
• What do you like best about it?	• Did you have any problems? What did you do?
• Anything else?	• Anything else?

Frameworks for developing content

Encouraging Participation

Activity-based language skills develop most effectively in classrooms where children are confident and motivated to share.

The following points should be noted:

- Children's motivation to share is likely to be greater if there is a purpose for sharing. Reinforce the benefits of sharing and discussion; for example:
  We heard about lots of different ways of building a solar-powered house. You might like to include some of these ideas in your project.
- Activity-based sharing sessions should not have a sole focus on performance. Emphasise the value of participation; for example:
  We've had everyone involved in speaking and listening in today's sharing circle. When everyone joins in we share a lot of different ideas.
- Speaking and listening are both important roles. Reinforce the value of each; for example:
  Ben has finished sharing and now he's listening while others have a turn. Listening will help him to learn how the other group tried to solve the problem.
- Children should be given opportunities for informal sharing. Allocate a time during the week for selecting work examples; for example:
  Choose something you would like to share. It might be something you completed today or something from your writing folder.

Children Who Are Reluctant to Share

Most children are naturally motivated to share their experiences and will participate spontaneously during activity-based sharing activities. However, when children are reluctant to participate, look for a reason and select an appropriate strategy to develop their confidence or skills. For example, some children have experienced a rich language environment at home and in their own community, but may be inhibited by the more formal atmosphere and different language patterns of school. Initially, they will need to listen to a wide range of language models within an enriched classroom environment. Quite often these children will begin to participate after observing how their peers interact and contribute ideas. It is extremely important that the language and cultural experiences these children bring to school are highly valued by the teacher and by other children.

Children who are anxious or who have a low self-esteem will generally avoid talking during whole-class activities. These children will benefit from small-group sessions where the teacher can provide a higher level of support and facilitation.

When selecting strategies, teachers need to strike a balance between the formality of the activity and the individual needs of the children. Careful observation of children in a variety of sharing situations will assist teachers to structure appropriate support for reluctant speakers.

Differences Between Newstelling and Activity-based Sharing

Newstelling is the structured activity-based language activity most commonly observed in classrooms. It draws on children's natural motivation to share experiences and, with skilful teacher facilitation, can be used to develop a range of social and literacy skills (refer *Language and Literacy* chapter of this book). A newstelling presentation requires children to:

- reconstruct an experience by reflecting on the key elements
- sequence the events in logical order
- include *when, who, where* and *what* in the recount
- judge the level of information required by the audience

At times, teachers may observe children who have difficulty dealing with the abstract elements of a recount, i.e. *when, who, where, what, why*. Other children may attempt to recount an experience with limited knowledge of the associated vocabulary. When this occurs the audience is required to visualise the experience from incomplete or partially-elaborated information. Children who have difficulty planning and presenting news items may have more success with activity-based sharing sessions that give the teacher greater control over the experience and the manner in which it is described. For example, during a science lesson, the teacher can make decisions about:

- *Organisation*   - work in pairs, problem solve together
- *Vocabulary*   - introduce *metamorphosis, erosion, granite, igneous*
- *Sharing*   - Group 1 - describe model and materials used
                      Group 2 - explain how model was produced
                      Group 3 - evaluate effectiveness of model

The value of this approach lies in the children being actively engaged in the experience within the classroom. They participate in the activity, have teacher support where necessary, practise appropriate vocabulary and share their discoveries at the conclusion of the session. In addition, activity-based lessons that produce models or displays, provide visual cues to assist children to make the links between what is being described and what has been produced.

Differences Between Newstelling and Activity-based Sharing	
• Children describe an event experienced outside the classroom.	• Children describe an activity completed in class.
• The teacher has no control over the experience.	• The teacher can support children and manipulate the experience to ensure success.
• Newstelling components are abstract: *When, Who, Where, What, Why*.	• Activity-based sharing components relate to: *name, attributes, function, stages in production*.
• The teacher has little control over vocabulary.	• The teacher can introduce subject-specific vocabulary.
• The audience must visualise the experience.	• The audience can see the finished item.

Assessment

An integral part of any teaching process should include ongoing monitoring and evaluation of children's performances. This approach is particularly important when implementing activity-based sharing since the dynamic and interactive nature of the strategies demands different levels of support for different skills and ability levels.

Formal individual or group assessment can be completed using the rating scale on the following page. The scale identifies four aspects of activity-based sharing performance:

Content – the type of content children produce when they share;
Language Structures – the vocabulary and sentence structures used;
Independence – the amount of teacher prompting and support needed for sharing;
Participation – children's motivation to share.

The continuum of indicators on pages 20–21 traces the development of activity-based sharing skills. Teachers may wish to use the indicators to assess children's control of the language of activity-based sharing.

Activity-based Sharing: Rating Scale

Name: _____

Date: _____

Class: _____

Area	1	2	3	4
Content	• No language initiated spontaneously	• Simple labelling of item or activity	• More detailed description • Explanations included˙	• Reflective comment
Language Structures	• Single word responses or incomplete sentences	• Complete but simple sentences • May follow stereotyped sentence pattern and make repetitive use of '*and*' • Non-specific vocabulary	• More complex sentence structure with range of connectors, *e.g. but, if, when* • specific vocabulary used to refer to item or experience	• Sentences linked to create 'text-like' effect
Independence	• Sharing totally prompted	• Needs frequent prompts • Closed prompts used, e.g. *What did you use?*	• Needs some prompts • Open prompts e.g. *Can you explain more?*	• Shares independently
Participation	• Avoids turn or has refusal behaviours	• Has turn at teacher request • Non-verbal signs of discomfort	• Bids for turn • Has appropriate non-verbal behaviours	• Approaches sharing with confidence and enjoyment • High level of interaction with audience

ACTIVITY-BASED SHARING

Sharing activities encourage children to become active participants in learning through meaningful speaking and listening activities across the curriculum.

Indicators

BEGINNING

The children require teacher support to initiate information related to the experience.

DEVELOPING

The child provides a general description of the experience.

CONSOLIDATING

The child uses teacher facilitation to provide a detailed description of an experience or explanation of a completed task.

EXPANDING

The child engages in meaningful sharing sessions that range from informal activity-based talk to formal classroom presentations that require a higher level of reflection and planning.

Text Content and Organisation
The child:

- requires extensive teacher support to initiate any language related to the experience or task
- sits/stands by the listener but does not communicate
- makes one or two word statements, e.g. *Painting. My building.*

Text Content and Organisation
The child:

- initiates a simple statement about the activity or item, e.g. *We made a boat. This is what I did.*
- relies on teacher prompts to extend the description, e.g. through questions or comments
- follows a simple, practised presentation process, e.g. introduces and labels an item, describes main features and stages in production

Text Content and Organisation
The child:

- initiates a detailed description of the activity or item, e.g. nature of task, and features of completed item
- responds to teacher support in providing more detail or evaluative comments
- reflects on task, plans and presents information in logical sequence

Text Content and Organisation
The child:

- outlines the purpose of the activity
- describes the main features of the item or activity
- explains how the task or item was completed, e.g. materials, steps, planning and decision making, problems and solutions
- reflects on the project, e.g. similar to a previous activity
- reflects on the process, e.g. what has been learned

Vocabulary and Sentence Structure
The child:

- uses single words or uncompleted sentences
- repeats phrases, makes false starts, includes hesitations
- uses limited vocabulary that may provide insufficient information for the listener
- uses simple conjunctions, e.g. *and, them*

Vocabulary and Sentence Structure
The child:

- uses complete but simple sentences, e.g. *I made this dinosaur.*
- begins to use language to link ideas together, e.g. *This is a story map. It's about a bear. He gets lost.*
- rephrases ideas, adds fillers, e.g. *um, ah*
- begins to incorporate general vocabulary, e.g. colour, size, shape
- uses stereotyped sentence pattern and repetitive use of *and*

Vocabulary and Sentence Structure
The child:

- uses more complex sentence structures with range of connectors, e.g. *and, but, so*
- uses language to link main components of sharing session, e.g. reflects, plans, presents key elements of task
- rephrases ideas, clarifies information
- uses specific vocabulary related to the experience or item, e.g. maths vocabulary when explaining a problem-solving task

Vocabulary and Sentence Structure
The child:

- links sentences to create a text-like effect
- presents ideas in a logical and cohesive sequence
- selects vocabulary to enhance or expand on the presentation
- elaborates or summarises information in response to listener needs
- varies sentence length for impact or interest

Responsiveness of Child as Speaker
The child:
- uses single words or uncompleted sentences
- repeats phrases, makes false starts, includes hesitations
- uses limited vocabulary that may provide insufficient information for the listener
- uses simple conjunctions, e.g. *and, them*

Responsiveness of Child as Listener
The child:
- shows minimal response to the information provided
- asks questions that relate to established information
- is inattentive or passive or both
- interrupts with unrelated comments

Responsiveness of Child as Speaker
The child:
- responds to teacher support to participants in sharing
- begins to adapt language to suit different audience, e.g. spontaneous sharing with partner or simple planning and presentation to small group
- responds to teacher prompts when extending description or explanation of task, e.g. *What else did you use?*
- uses appropriate rate and volume

Responsiveness of Child as Listener
The child:
- uses stereotype comments or questions, e.g. *It's nice. What did you use?*
- initiates general comments related to the task, e.g. *I made one of those, too*
- shows an interest in the sharing session by making comments or questioning
- asks questions that show an understanding of the task, e.g. *Why did it break?*

Responsiveness of Child as Speaker
The child:
- displays general mannerisms that signal composure and confidence, e.g. sweeping eye movements, adjusting rate and volume
- bids for an opportunity to share
- interacts with audience by adding or clarifying information
- reflects, plans and presents information in informal situations, e.g. small group sharing
- plans and presents information in formal situations, with teacher support in formal situations, e.g. interclass presentations

Responsiveness of Child as Listener
The child:
- interacts with the speaker by following the description or explanation
- monitors the description or explanation and asks follow-up questions
- makes comments that show an understanding of the steps involved in completing the task, e.g. *Our bridge broke, too. We didn't use enough support.*
- asks questions to gain or clarify information, e.g. *Why did you use triangle shapes?*

Responsiveness of Child as Speaker
The child:
- demonstrates awareness of different audience needs, e.g. adjusts language style to suit class or assembly item
- demonstrates a high level of interaction with the audience, e.g. monitors audience response, adds or summarises information, responds to question
- demonstrates a high level of reflection, planning, and presentation
- reflects and comments on both the product and process, e.g. the success of the completed model and changes to the process next time
- performs confidently in both informal and formal situations

Responsiveness of Child as Listener
The child:
- shows a high level of involvement, e.g. offers solutions or evaluative comments
- makes links between personal experience and description of task or experience
- questions show high level of understanding of process involved in the task, e.g. Did you find you had to go back and start again when the first part of the experiment didn't work?
- Makes generalisations from information provided, e.g. *Triangles must be the best shape to use when you are building a bridge.*

Section 2:

Discussion

Group discussion and interaction challenge children's thinking, encouraging them to consider issues from different points of view. They teach children how to use communication skills to resolve conflicts in positive ways. The ability to compromise and reach consensus is an important life skill.

Group work develops cooperative attitudes and behaviours. Children learn the value of sharing and helping. In group situations children must coordinate effort and divide labour. They have the opportunity to experience different roles and responsibilities. Participation in group discussion develops flexibility and tolerance of individual differences.

Group discussion is a strategy for clarifying understanding. With peers, children can express ideas they are tentative or unsure about. Group work develops problem-solving and independent learning skills.

The Language of Discussion

Partner and group discussion make complex demands on speakers and listeners. Children are required to use language to create cohesion and group unity, coordinate group activity, and reach a more complete and objective understanding of the topic. Disagreeing and seeking consensus are also part of this discussion process.

In the classroom, teachers need to introduce a range of speaking and listening activities that develop discussion skills across the curriculum

- **to promote group cohesion**
  inviting other children to join in
  asking for or offering help
  giving praise and encouragement
  joking and making humorous comments

- **to coordinate group activities**
  calling for group attention, e.g. *Look at ...*
  giving instructions
  planning
  negotiating roles
  offering feedback and summarising comments

- **to explore topics creatively**
  offering ideas and opinions
  elaborating others' ideas
  disagreeing, challenging
  asking for clarification
  explaining, justifying

- **to encourage resolution and consensus**
  appealing to rules, authority
  persuading
  agreeing
  suggesting compromise

Contexts for Discussion

Coordinating ideas and opinions during group discussion requires a high degree of cooperation and flexibility. The partner and group discussion activities outlined here are most effective when implemented in a classroom where the values of sharing and cooperation are already established. In classrooms where this is not evident, non-productive conflicts often arise during group discussions.

The following social behaviours can be fostered by providing a range of contexts.

Group Identity
- Organise activities that create feelings of unity and group identity, such as shared projects or planning assembly items.
- Include socially-oriented events, such as excursions, camps or parties.

Awareness of Others
- Introduce 'Getting to know each other' activities such as learning about individuals' families, cultural backgrounds and languages and comment positively on individual differences.
- Invite people of various ages and backgrounds to describe their lifestyles or experiences.
- Take advantage of special events to recognise individual talents.

Sharing and Cooperation
- Provide practice in sharing tasks as soon as children begin school.
- Implement systems for sharing materials and reinforce helping and cooperative behaviours, drawing attention to the positive aspects of working with others.
- Organise children with particular knowledge and skills to teach other children and encourage children to share responsibilities and rewards.

Discussion and Negotiation
- Negotiate classroom rules and routines.
- Provide discussion time to resolve classroom conflicts, promoting participation by all class members.
- Discuss the communication and cooperative skills required to work with others.
- Create work spaces that encourage interaction and spend time reflecting on and discussing what was learned from group activities.
- Provide joint decision-making activities, such as class meetings, discussions and planning sessions.

Teaching Strategies

Promoting Conversation

Every classroom activity can be used to initiate conversation.

The following transcripts contrast conversations from two kindergarten classes. In the first example the children have limited opportunities to share and discuss as they are working. The small amount of language generated is directed to the adult, not to the other children.

Adult:	*Then the one you can see on top facing you… fold that towards the window. Now this one goes towards the window, right?*
Renee:	*Mrs S, I can do this one.*
Adult:	*(talking to another child)…Right, that one goes towards the window. Yes, that one goes first…keeping it nice and square.* *… Put this one towards the window. Put it in nicely. Try not to hurry.*
Natalie:	*My one is slipping.*
Adult:	*That has to go over to the window. Let me check that.*

Compare the example with the following illustration of kindergarten interaction during an art and crafts activity. On this occasion, the adult is seated with the children and completes the task in parallel with them. The conversation, both with the adult and with each other, is lively and interesting:

Emily:	*White glue! I haven't seen white glue.*
Janet:	*I've seen some white glue.*
Adult:	*Let's see. It's clear, isn't it? Not like the other white glue you use though. I'm going to stick mine on like a diamond, like this.*
Bradley:	*My rock is a different colour. What are you going to put in it?*
Adult:	*I don't know.*
Emily:	*Maybe your jewellery.*
Adult:	*A jewellery box! What a good idea. Or shells.*
Bradley:	*How could you make shells?*
Adult:	*I could collect some shells off the beach.*
Ryan:	*Are you going to decorate it on the other side? (to Bradley)*
Janet:	*And what about on the side there? Silly Billy.*

This example demonstrates how adults can promote children's conversation in a positive, enjoyable learning environment. Interaction of this kind facilitates both language and cognitive development.

Some of the following activities are outlined in greater detail in the *Activity-based Sharing* section of *Language of Social Interaction* and the *Partner Work* section of *Language and Thinking*.

- Partner Work
  Assign tasks that children need to complete together, such as collages or block constructions. This type of organisation generates lively, purposeful discussion, e.g. planning, giving instructions, describing, commenting (see *Partner Work* section).

- Table Work
  Sit at the children's table and join in their activity. It is important that you or the parent volunteer are not too intrusive and that you join in the conversation in a

natural way. Using the situation as a substitute 'lesson' tends to inhibit rather than facilitate conversation between children. It is also important that all questions are genuine, e.g. 'However did you manage to make that stay up?' and not 'What colour/shape/size is it?'

- 'Special Friend' Day
  Organise the children in pairs. During the day they do things together such as helping each other or sharing a favourite book.

- Picture Talk
  This is an alternative and interesting way of conducting a picture talk activity. When discussion has commenced, move away from the group, then return a short time later. Discussion does not stop when the teacher leaves. On the contrary, children often see this as a type of play activity, pointing out details and creating stories related to the picture. The more spontaneous and open-ended the task, the better.

Partner Discussion

Partner discussion is a strategy that develops children's ability to initiate and sustain discussion on a chosen topic. For less confident speakers, it provides a practice context in which there is no pressure to 'perform' for the group. The strategy also encourages more tolerant and supportive listening from children who usually dominate verbal exchanges in the classroom.

Most classrooms have children who lack confidence and skills in initiating talk. Not only is this a barrier to a child's social development but it also deprives the group of the opportunity to share in the experiences and ideas of individual members.

The following is an extract of interaction from a partner discussion:

Teacher:	*OK, Partner 2 is going to go first this time.*
	Partner 2, tell your partner what you usually do when you get home from school.
Child 1:	*I ride my bike down the street to my friend's and we play video games. He's got a new computer.*
Teacher:	*Partner 1, it's your turn now.*
Child 2:	*I have something to eat.*
Child 1:	*Like what?*
Child 2:	*Biscuits, and sometimes I have peanut butter on bread.*
Child 1:	*Do you have anything to drink?*
Child 2:	*Orange juice 'cos I'm not allowed to have Coke all the time.*
Teacher:	*OK. Who would like to share some of the things they found out about what their partner does when they get home from school?*
Child 2:	*Jason goes to his friend's place and they play video games.*
Teacher:	*Did he tell you what his favourite game was…?*

During partner discussion sessions, turn-taking and selecting topics are directed by the teacher. This structured approach can be modified as children gain skill and independence. In the beginning it provides a supportive framework for children who have difficulty initiating conversation independently. As they become more confident, children interact with a variety of partners to maximise the effects of peer modelling and to experience feedback from different listeners.

Procedure

1 Organise pairs and allocate each person a number, either 1 or 2.
2 Explain the activity: *We're going to do some partner discussion work. In a minute I am going to ask you to talk about the special topic I've chosen for today. This is a time when we have to remember the rules we have for good speaking and listening in the class.*
3 Check that children are sitting in an appropriate place to carry on a conversation with their partner.
4 Introduce the topic and nominate one child in each pair to share ideas first, e.g. *OK, Partner 1, I want you to tell your partner what you did before you came to school this morning.*
5 Allow a few minutes for children to complete sharing, then instruct the other child to have a turn.
6 Invite two or three children to share their partner's information with the whole group.
7 Introduce the next conversational 'starter'. Repeat the procedure three or four times with a new discussion topic or extensions of the previous topic. Discontinue the session if the children are losing interest in the activity.
8 Encourage the courtesy of thanking each partner at the end of the session.
9 When children are familiar with the partner discussion procedure, allow about five minutes at the end of the session for discussion of self-initiated topics.

Ideas for Partner Discussion Topics

- Exchanging personal information
  Tell your partner about …
  … where you live
  … one person in your family
  … what you usually do when you get home from school
  … people and places your family visits

- Sharing likes and dislikes
  Share with your partner …
  … two things you like to do at lunchtime, on the weekend, on the holidays
  … what your favourite TV program is and why
  … what your favourite time of the day is and why
  … the thing you most like to do when it is raining
  … the favourite thing you own and why

- Recounting experiences
  What do you remember about …
  … what you did before you were old enough to go to school?
  … what you did on your last birthday?
  … where you went last Christmas?
  … the last film you saw?

- Expressing opinions
  Share with your partner …
  … what makes you angry, e.g. when playing a game
  … what you think about kids' programs on TV
  … what you think about the books in the school library
  … how you would feel if all the trees around the school oval were cut down

- Self-esteem
  Tell your partner …
  … some things you are good at doing
  … one thing you would like to learn to do and why
  … something that you like about him or her
  … something you could do together at lunchtime

- Describing and explaining
  Think about how to explain to your partner …
  … a walk down your street, around your backyard, through your house… What can you see?
  … your favourite room in your house… What would you like to change about your house?
  … a game and how to play it
  … your favourite sandwich and how to make it

- Swapping stories and jokes
Tell your partner …
… *about the book you have out of the library at the moment*
… *a joke*
… *a sad story about a giraffe whose neck was too short*

- Using your imagination
Share with your partner …
… *what you would choose if you could buy three new things for your bedroom*
… *what you would do if someone told you to have a lazy day*
… *what animal you would choose to turn into and why*
… *what the world would be like if you slept for a hundred years and then woke up*
… *what birthday present you would give a baby*

Teaching Points

- Begin with conversational topics that are concrete and within the child's experience.
- For children who initiate little information, provide structure when introducing topics; for example:
Choose one person in your family and tell your partner about him or her. You might tell how old the person is, his or her names, what jobs he/she does around the house, or things this person likes to watch on TV.
- Reinforce speaking and listening courtesies; for example
Melissa and Karen, I really like the way you have turned so you are facing each other. When you look at the person it lets her/him know that you're interested in what is being said.
- Encourage children to use questions to get additional information from their partner. Model discussion and follow-up at sharing time; for example:
Did you ask Michael how old his brother is? Is his brother older or younger than yours?
- Encourage children to elaborate ideas; for example:
Partner 1, I'm going to give you an extra minute to add one more idea. You might want to add a new idea or explain something you already told your partner.
- Give children the experience of working with different partners. This exposes them to a variety of peer modelling and feedback.

Small-group Discussion

Teaching Group Roles

In this section, discussion is introduced through the establishment of roles and the clarification of what is expected of the group and its members. In an effective group organisation, individuals are dependent on each other to achieve a common goal. The responsibility for directing the task and contributing ideas is shared equally among its members, although some participants may assume specific roles.

In the classroom, children also need the opportunity to practise and refine a range of roles to develop social and communication skills through discussion. Although the process requires careful planning and monitoring, the investment of time and teaching expertise is worthwhile. Developing an awareness and understanding of group processes gives children an important strategy for independent learning.

One of the difficulties in setting up successful small-group discussion sessions is ensuring that individuals are participating equally. Some individuals withdraw because they are self-conscious and anxious about how other people will judge them. Others dominate discussions, assuming control of the group's actions and decisions.

Procedure

1 Begin with a discussion of the roles children will be assigned in their groups. Each group may include:

A **manager**	– *who watches the time; summarises where the group is up to; makes sure everyone understands what the task is*
An **encourager**	– *who makes sure everyone is having a turn; asks people to give their opinion; praises others' ideas; encourages people to keep going*
A **recorder**	– *who writes down group's ideas; asks questions to check what people mean*
A **reporter**	– *who reports the group's idea back to the class*

Brainstorm some of the things that these people might say to each other while performing these roles (see example of children's brainstorming on page 31).

Stress that *all* group members are responsible for helping out with ideas.

2 Organise children in groups of four. Allocate roles or ask children to negotiate these in their groups.

3 Ask one child representing each role to re-explain his/her task to the class. This revision is useful when children have gone into their own groups, and before they start the discussion activity.

4 Introduce the activity that is to be completed by the groups (see *Ideas for Small Group Discussion*, page 32).

5 Observe children's interaction during the small-group activity. Assist groups that are having difficulty. Note any examples of interaction that demonstrate children's understanding of their assigned roles.

6 Ask reporters from each of the groups to share their group's work with the whole class. Invite discussion and questions.

7 Share with the group examples of effective interaction that you observed with the group, e.g. *Matthew noticed that his group was slowing down and he said to them, 'Keep going'.*

8 Encourage children to reflect on the experience; for example:

- *What was something you did that helped your group?*
- *What is something you would do differently next time?*
- *Did you notice things that other people did in your group that helped?*
- *What did you learn from doing this with other people?*

Encourager

Hey, it's your turn!

Try to make your voice louder.

That's all right. It doesn't matter.

That's a really good idea!

Keep trying.

Reporter

What does this word say?

What can I say about this bit?

Have you got any ideas?

Is that OK?

What's the introduction?

Manager

Does everyone understand?

OK. So what we've decided is …

Right, we've finished the first one.

We've got five minutes left.

Recorder

We've got eight so far.

One at a time, please!

Could you please slow down?

How do you write that?

Ideas for Small-group Discussion

Selection of discussion activities is an important aspect of planning small-group instruction. It is best to begin with simple activities so children are free to monitor what is happening to the group and can think about their group role. Later, introduce activities that elicit different ideas and opinions, so children have to work harder at achieving consensus.

The group discussion ideas listed below can be adapted to suit all Year levels. Brainstorming is usually an effective starting point and should be continued until children develop an understanding of group roles. Ranking or story cloze should not be introduced until group cooperation and discussion are well established.

When groups of children have gained confidence through practice, it is often useful to stop them in the middle of a session and ask them to reflect on what has happened, what is happening and what direction they predict they will take.

- Brainstorming
  All of you are going by car to the beach. Think of all the safety rules you may need to follow from the time you leave home until the time you leave the beach.

- Making choices
  Grandma is sick in bed. What three items would you take to her if you were given this list to choose from?

walking-stick	*rug*	*apples*
chocolates	*book*	*hamburger*
perfume	*flowers*	*vitamin pills*

- Ranking
  You are going on a school camp on the edge of the desert. From this list of items, choose four extra things to take. Just in case you can't take all four items (there may be too much luggage), rank your chosen items in order, giving reasons for your choice.

- Story cloze
  Here is a cartoon. As you can see, the speech bubbles are empty. What your group has to do is to decide what is happening in the story and what the characters would be saying to each other.

At the end of a session it is important to give children time and opportunity to discuss the strategies they or others use to break into the conversation; to assert a point of view, to avoid commitment, etc.

Linking to writing
Group discussion provides opportunities for children to practise note-taking skills. It is important that roles are rotated so that all children have a turn at being the recorder. Children should be encouraged to ask for help from other group members for sentence ideas and spelling.

Sick Grandma

What present would you choose. Why?

a blanket chocolate flowers books walking stick jumper cream cake

1. a blanket   keep warm in bed because she might have a flu or cold.

2. books   to keep her occupied.

3. walking stick   she might need a walking stick because of hunch back.

Thankyou my dears !

Example of note-taking from a group discussion.

Teaching Points

- Use mixed-ability groups, including children who have a good understanding of the task. It is also important that children learn to interact successfully with children outside their friendship group.
- Social development plays an important part in the school curriculum; for example: *Today you practised ways of working together. Are there any things you learned that you think you could do at home?*
- Give specific feedback. This helps to clarify and reinforce children's understanding of group roles; for example:
  Jenny, I heard you ask someone in the group to repeat what was said because you hadn't understood what was meant. That's a good thing for the recorder to do before she/he writes something down. And it means that other people in the group might think of questions they want to ask, too.
- Brainstorm verbal and non-verbal strategies that children can use; for example:
  How could you get people to talk more?
  You could …
  … invite them to have a turn
  … say an idea and get them to tell you what they think about it
  … ask them a question
  … look at them and wait
  … encourage them when they join in.
- Use observations to highlight areas that may need a special focus. For example, if there is negative interaction, provide practice in giving positive feedback. Alternatively, think of ideas to add to what another child has said.

Informal Debate

This section features a simple strategy that can be used as a bridge to the more formal debating activities of upper primary. At this stage, formal debating procedure is not introduced, but children can become familiar with some of the processes involved in constructing, presenting and defending a point of view.

In small groups, children discuss the debate topic and generate reasons for choosing the affirmative or negative position. When presenting their case to the whole group, children are required to substantiate their opinions and must also evaluate the arguments that have been presented by others.

The modelling provided by this activity is particularly valuable for children who are impulsive in forming opinions and making decisions. For all children, the activity provides an opportunity to practise logical thinking through talking.

Procedure

1 Organise small groups and assign roles of Manager, Encourager, Recorder, Reporter (see page 30).
2 Introduce a debate topic, such as 'Summer is the best season'.
3 Instruct groups to discuss the topic and record reasons for a 'yes' or 'no' response.
4 Reconvene the whole group. Each group presents ideas that are recorded on a master sheet.
5 Summarise the points that have been discussed on the affirmative and negative sides.
6 Conduct a classroom vote to decide the outcome of the debate.

Ideas for debate topics

Debates are an effective way of consolidating social studies or literature themes. When children are familiar with the concept of debating they may suggest their own topics for discussion. Here are a few suggestions.

- *Summer is the best season*
- *Big families are best*
- *It's good to live in the same place all your life*
- *'Many friends' are better than 'one best friend'*
- *The Gingerbread Man deserved to be caught*
- *Footballs should be round*

Linking to Writing

The group discussion component of this strategy requires some note-taking. Group discussion sheets can be redrafted in a neat form after the activity to provide a group report. Alternatively, the affirmative and negative sides of the argument can be summarised in a whole-group modelled writing session.

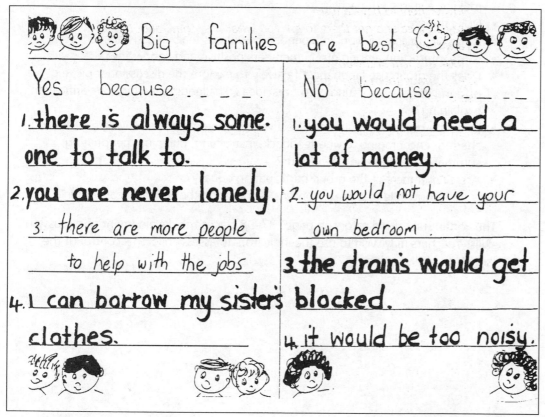

Big families are best.

Yes because	No because
1. there is always some. one to talk to.	1. you would need a lot of money.
2. you are never lonely.	2. you would not have your own bedroom.
3. there are more people to help with the jobs	3. the drains would get blocked.
4. I can borrow my sister's clothes.	4. it would be too noisy.

Example of Year 2 Summary

Teaching Points

- Reinforce effective role-taking (see pages 29–30).
- Encourage whole-group discussion when presenters are sharing their group's ideas. Encourage the audience to think of counter-arguments for the ideas they are hearing, e.g. *But being able to watch more TV because you can't go outside gets a bit boring.*
- Model how to summarise when recording in the whole-group session and summing up at the end. Solicit children's ideas about how to record information in brief point form.
- Train presenters to mark off points that have been presented by the previous speaker.

Assessment

Developing children's oral language skills requires a reflective teaching approach. It involves skilful observation of children's performance and sensitive structuring and support based on these observations. Teaching group discussion skills is an example of this 'diagnostic' teaching approach.

Group discussion provides an opportunity to step back and observe children's skills when they are working independently. On the basis of these observations, teachers identify communication skills that need development. These areas then become a focus for group discussion during which alternative strategies are brainstormed and demonstrated. In this way the strategy becomes tailored to meet the specific needs of each group.

What To Look For

- Does the group reach mutual agreement about what has to be done before making a start to the activity?
- Does the group stay on task?
- Is the group able to work independently without teacher assistance?
- Is the interaction among group members positive and cooperative?
- Does the group use language effectively to explore the discussion topic, e.g. offering ideas, elaborating on others' ideas, challenging, asking for clarification, explaining?
- Does the group use language effectively to coordinate the activity, e.g. helping, sharing, encouraging, giving feedback, instructing, planning, negotiating, summarising, regulating behaviour?
- Are all members of the group participating equally?
- Is the group able to achieve consensus and bring the task to a conclusion?

The continuum of indicators on pages 37–38 traces the development of discussion skills. Teachers may wish to use the indicators to assess children's control of the language of discussion.

DISCUSSION

Indicators

Discussion involves interaction by small or large groups to reach a deeper understanding of topics.
Language is used to clarify thinking, gain new knowledge, and express ideas and opinions.

BEGINNING

The child requires teacher support to engage in simple conversational topics.

Text Content and Organisation
The child:

- initiates little information
- relies on teacher or adult support to maintain conversational interaction

Vocabulary and Sentence Structure
The child:

- makes simple statements related to common experiences, classroom activities, concrete objects, etc.
- repeats phrases, makes false starts, has incomplete utterances, includes hesitations
- uses limited vocabulary that may provide insufficient information for the listener
- uses simple conjunctions, e.g. *and, then*

DEVELOPING

The child begins to engage in structured partner discussions that require teacher support to initiate and sustain topics.

Text Content and Organisation
The child:

- initiates and sustains discussion on topics within his/her experience
- relies on teacher direction to select a topic for discussion
- needs teacher facilitation to move between role of speaker and listener

Vocabulary and Sentence Structure
The child:

- makes general comments about a chosen topic, including information that has a common interest to the group
- uses simple sentence structures, rephrases, ideas, adds fillers, e.g. *um, ah*
- begins to incorporate vocabulary that enables the listener to interpret the message
- uses simple conjunctions, e.g. *and, then, next, but*

CONSOLIDATING

The child interacts successfully in informal, small-group discussions.

Text Content and Organisation
The child:

- expresses opinions and under- standings of a limited range of topics through conversation, discussion or argument
- uses language to demonstrate different roles within a group, e.g. manager, reporter

Vocabulary and Sentence Structure
The child:

- makes comments and expresses opinions about a range of classroom- initiated topics
- uses extended sentences to express ideas and opinions
- selects vocabulary to enhance ideas or opinions
- incorporates more complex conjunctions, e.g. *however, so, because, although*

EXPANDING

The child is actively engaged as both speaker and listener, in informal and formal discussion groups.

Text Content and Organisation
The child:

- explores and expresses opinions and ideas related to concrete or abstract experiences
- uses a range of communication styles, both informal and formal, e.g. summarising a group discussion, presenting a point of view in a debate

Vocabulary and Sentence Structure
The child:

- presents ideas and opinions spontaneously in response to the topic or other speaker's contributions
- varies sentence construction or length for impact
- uses varied or specific vocabulary to express ideas and opinions
- elaborates or summarises information to express a point of view, clarify thinking or gain new knowledge

DISCUSSION

BEGINNING

Responsiveness of Child as Speaker
The child:

- displays limited understanding of the interactive nature of the conversation or discussion, e.g. shows no response or offers little elaboration or detail
- requires adult intervention or support to sustain a conversation
- adds few comments or questions in response to others' information

Responsiveness of Child as Listener
The child:

- shows minimal response to topics initiated by others
- shows limited understanding of need to listen and respond during an interaction
- is unaware of questioning as a strategy for gaining or clarifying information

DEVELOPING

Responsiveness of Child as Speaker
The child:

- begins to make comments or ask relevant questions to extend ideas
- clarifies comments by rephrasing or repeating information, e.g. *I mean ...*
- responds to feedback from others by repeating or rephrasing information, adding further explanation
- takes turns, asks questions, responds, listens, during interactions

Responsiveness of Child as Listener
The child:

- responds to the topic by initiating ideas or comments within his/her experience
- responds to the topic by asking questions
- seeks clarification when something is not understood, e.g. *Do you mean ...?*
- interrupts or interacts in an appropriate manner
- seeks rights as a listener in an appropriate manner regarding volume and viewing, e.g. *I can't see/hear*—stands up

CONSOLIDATING

Responsiveness of Child as Speaker
The child:

- asks for and provides explanations or reasons
- clarifies information by repeating, rephrasing or extending information
- elaborates ideas and information in response to group's questions or comments
- takes turns using appropriate tone, volume and conventions
- expands on others' ideas or comments
- negotiates group role and reaches consensus on nature of discussion or task

Responsiveness of Child as Listener
The child:

- listens actively by identifying and commenting on the topic
- asks for further information or explanation to clarify arguments or ideas expressed by others
- expresses ideas or opinions based on new information or ideas gained
- interrupts and interacts appropriately in informal and formal group situations
- beginning to be critical but response is not always appropriate, e.g. listener is right, not speaker

EXPANDING

Responsiveness of Child as Speaker
The child:

- confidently volunteers ideas, information and opinions
- justifies and substantiates opinions and arguments
- elaborates and expands own point of view
- paraphrases others' comments to clarify viewpoints
- questions to clarify others' opinions
- invites other group members to contribute
- negotiates group roles to ensure task is understood
- interacts using appropriate speech style, volume, tone, etc.

Responsiveness of Child as Listener
The child:

- shows a high level of involvement, e.g. elaborates on others' ideas, challenges opinions or asks for clarification
- monitors the discussion by asking questions, arguing or expressing different points of view
- monitors own understandings by paraphrasing or summarising information
- listens and responds constructively to ideas or points of view

Section 3:

Social Conventions

The social and cultural group to which children belong has a significant effect on the way they communicate and behave. Children's backgrounds will determine the language (e.g. Italian, Greek, Indonesian, Khyma, English) they speak, their attitudes towards language use, the scope of experiences they have had, and the variety of people with whom they have interacted.

Any group of children beginning school will display a range of backgrounds, language styles and expectations of how they should interact in the classroom. Social and cultural factors will strongly influence how they communicate with teachers and peers. Some children may come to school with a limited knowledge of English but a profound knowledge of one or two other languages. Others may have experienced few social contacts beyond their home environment. Many will be unaware of the variation in the style of language that is appropriate in school situations, such as the playground, the classroom or a school assembly.

Teachers need to ensure that children have the opportunity to respond effectively and confidently to the demands of both the classroom and the wider environment. Children will need to learn that a style of language and behaviour used may be suitable in one situation but not for another. Those children who are shy or lacking confidence may need to work individually, or in a small group, with a supportive adult in order to improve their communication skills. Non-English speaking children will need to hear and speak with a variety of English-speaking models as well as people from their own or other language backgrounds. On occasions, teachers may also need to intervene to correct or model particular aspects of a speech, such as pronunciation or word usage in a natural context that makes sense to the children.

The Language of Social Conventions

The people with whom children interact exert a considerable influence on the way they use language to communicate. In the classroom, the audience moves from child to child, child to children, child to teacher or child to adults. Children's ability to communicate effectively in each of these situations will depend on their confidence, familiarity with the audience and opportunities they have had to develop appropriate language for a range of audiences.

Young children, particularly those beginning kindergarten, may lack confidence when they are introduced to unfamiliar people in a new environment. Shyness, dependency, inappropriate attention-seeking behaviour, avoidance, non-participation, a lack of responsiveness or increased physical aggression may lead to poor social or communication skills. While these behaviours may be linked to developmental delays or emotional problems, a more common cause usually relates to the child's different range of experiences and lack of opportunity to develop some level of independence within the kindergarten or early school setting.

In order to develop children's social and communication skills, teachers need to build on the language resources children already possess. Fortunately, most children have established good basic communication skills before they commence school and the home to school transition period is relatively smooth. A successful language program should provide a variety of challenging activities to extend these understandings and develop children's abilities to communicate across all curriculum areas.

This component identifies three areas that can be developed or extended to promote effective classroom communication and participation. Ideas can be adapted or developed to suit all year levels and abilities. They are most effective when introduced in a caring and supportive classroom where the rules and expectations of behaviour promote, rather than hinder, interaction and learning.

- **Developing Communication Skills**
  – *awareness of context, purpose and audience*

- **Speaking and Listening Courtesies**
  – *appropriate behaviour for different situations*
  – *negotiating classroom rules*

- **Problem solving in the classroom**
  – *problem solving social situations*
  – *formal and informal talk*
  – *spoken to written language*

Contexts for Using Social Conventions

A typical classroom day involves many incidental teaching moments, such as waiting expectantly until a greeting is acknowledged or reminding a child to wait until the end of an instruction. Language changes in response to the purposes and demands placed on the speaker. Children learn to communicate effectively by experiencing situations in which they both use and hear others use language for a variety of purposes. In the classroom, children need practice in interacting with peers, teachers, well-known adults and with people who are unfamiliar to them. The more opportunities children have to communicate with a variety of language models, the more flexible and sophisticated their language will become.

Teachers can stimulate the growth of effective communication skills by providing a range of learning situations inside and outside the classroom. Children need to interact with others and express their understandings in partner, small-group and whole-class activities; for example

- *asking the child to make a choice between two items*
- *'forgetting' to give the child an item so they must ask for it*
- *giving the child someone else's work rather than their own so they have to draw the mistake to the teacher's attention*
- *asking the child to relay a simple message within the classroom, such as, 'Can you ask John to come here?'*
- *giving the child a special task or responsibility*
- *asking the child to teach something to another child*
- *asking the child to share a book or a picture*

Teaching Strategies

Communication Skills

Speaking and Listening Corner

Establish a speaking and listening corner and encourage children to take part in a variety of activities such as story telling, conversing or discussing items on a display table. Include books, photographs, charts, tapes, construction materials, puppets, telephones and items to stimulate curiosity.

Discussion with Teacher

Encourage children to talk, ask questions, express ideas and opinions. Discuss work, interests and personal experiences or problems.

Talking to Adults

Include parents or community members in classroom activities. An increase in child-adult interactions will provide a variety of correct models of language and will assist children's learning and their ability to communicate with a range of people.

Relaying Messages and Information

Give children responsibility for relaying messages or conveying information to people inside and outside the classroom, e.g. other children, teachers, office staff, principal, parents. Model how to listen attentively and plan for conveying information to the listener. If necessary, brainstorm and chart rules for giving and receiving messages. Initially, allow children to practise the message before delivering it.

Developing Communication Skills

To give a good message I need to :

- Look at the person .

- Speak clearly .

- Use a suitable voice for the distance .

- Remember not to speak too fast .

To receive a message I need to :

- Look at the person .

- Listen carefully .

- Ask about anything I don't understand .

- Repeat the message .

- Write parts down I think I might forget .

Examples of charts for delivering and receiving messages

Conversations

Stimulate purposeful conversations in the classroom by introducing topics, raising issues, asking questions or reading books etc. Reinforce social behaviours such as listening to others, respecting different opinions, reacting courteously and interrupting in an appropriate way.

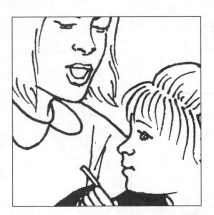

Discussions

Discussions can be formal or informal to serve both a social and learning function. Through discussion activities children learn acceptable group behaviour. They also have opportunities to communicate their opinions, ideas and understandings.

Discussion groups should be organised so children are actively involved as both speakers and listeners. The number in the group should allow all children to participate, initially with the teacher facilitating discussion, and ultimately as an independent group. (See *Discussion* section beginning on page 22 for instructional strategies.)

Interviews

Conduct group questioning sessions before introducing one-to-one interviews. Have the children generate and refine appropriate questions, then role play the interview with the teacher or other adult. Use this trial interview as a strategy for discussing, reflecting upon and evaluating the quality of questions and effectiveness of children's interview techniques. (The *Inquiry* section of the *Language and Thinking* Chapter beginning on page 149 outlines specific strategies for developing interview skills.)

Reports

Reports should involve children in recalling, sequencing and summarising information for presentation to an audience. In the classroom, children may report on group discussions, activities, personal experiences or aspects of learning across the curriculum. Initially, teachers will need to assist children to select and organise information for the report. (The *Activity-based Sharing* section beginning on page 2 outlines strategies for developing reporting skills.)

Non-verbal Communication

Observe features of non-verbal communication in different situations, e.g. in groups, in conversation, drama presentations or television advertisements. Discuss the role of this type of communication and its importance in promoting effective communication. Identify particular features such as whole body movements, facial gestures, hand movements and eye contact. Introduce activities that can be enhanced through non-verbal gestures, e.g. reading and story telling, jokes, riddles, giving directions or explaining a procedure. Make sure that classroom expectations do not infringe cultural norms.

Non-verbal Communication in the Media

Listen to, and compare, radio and television programs, e.g. news reports, advertisements, talk-back shows. Identify the nature and role of non-verbal communication in television broadcasts. When children are familiar with the content of the broadcast, turn down the sound and focus on gestures. Discuss the importance of non-verbal communication in persuading, conveying emotions, expressing opinions or establishing credibility.

What to look for

Do the Children:

- **approach people confidently?**
- **acknowledge that someone has spoken to them?**
- **establish eye contact?**
- **request attention verbally?**
- **express needs and wants, e.g. request assistance, seek permission?**
- **assert themselves appropriately with peers?**
- **relay simple messages successfully?**
- **use a louder voice when required?**

Contexts for Speaking and Listening Courtesies

Language plays a vital role in the personal and social development of children. It enables them to gain an understanding of themselves and others, and strengthen social relationships. Children who are confident and articulate tend to become socially competent. Others, who lack confidence or self-esteem may not have the capacity to express themselves adequately, or may attempt to gain attention by displaying inappropriate behaviour in the classroom.

An increased awareness of the social roles of speaking and listening are best promoted in an environment that is characterised by mutual respect and acceptance. The following activities will help children develop social skills by strengthening their ability to communicate appropriately and effectively within a supportive environment.

Courtesy goes beyond artificial role playing in the classroom. Initially, teachers provide good models of respect, courtesy and politeness in order to lay the foundations for a cooperative and caring classroom environment. A classroom that respects the needs, ideas, opinions and language of others will generally have few behaviour problems. Children will be willing to accept classroom rules and will express their ideas and feelings, knowing they will be accepted and respected. They will also develop a positive self-image and take more responsibility for their own learning.

The simple courtesies of allowing others to speak, listening to what they have to say and generally valuing what is said, can be developed from kindergarten and promoted throughout the school years.

Behaviour for Different Situations

Role Playing Acceptable and Unacceptable Behaviours

Role playing familiar classroom situations will assist younger children to demonstrate acceptable speaking and listening behaviours.

Steps:

1 Create contrasting characters to represent acceptable and unacceptable behaviours, e.g. *'Mabel Manners'* and *'Rachel Rude'*. Make puppets or face masks for each character.
2 Model a role play in which the *'Rachel Rude'* character demonstrates inappropriate behaviours. After the role play ask children to identify these behaviours and brainstorm more appropriate alternatives.
3 Select children to role play the *'Mabel Manners'* character using the same scenario. This can be done as a whole group or partner activity.
4 Brainstorm polite words for a chart, e.g. *Sorry, Please excuse me, Thank you, Would you, Would it be all right if ...* Discuss appropriate classroom situations for using these terms.

Ideas for Role Play

- Approaching an adult and demanding glue
- Taking someone's pencil and leaving it on another table at the end of an activity
- Neglecting to acknowledge a greeting
- Interrupting during a news session
- Forgetting to thank someone who has been of assistance
- Being careless and knocking over someone else's construction
- Arguing or fighting in the playground

Additional Activities

- Read books that highlight the themes of feelings or mutual respect.
- Write scenarios with the children based on the *Rachel Rude* or *Mabel Manners* characters.
- Introduce drama activities incorporating the puppets or masks of these characters.

Negotiating Classroom Rules

Discuss and negotiate classroom rules as a strategy for clarifying acceptable classroom behaviour and encouraging children to take responsibility for their own actions.

Listening

Discuss listening factors that contribute to effective and courteous listening in a variety of situations, e.g. with a partner, in a group, as a whole class. Observe and monitor listening habits over a period of time and discuss the information; for example:

- some children only listen intermittently during group work

- little value is placed on each other's comments
- children don't show an interest in others' comments by asking follow-up questions
- the teacher may not give a clear purpose for listening

As a group, devise and chart a set of rules that the children feel should apply when listening to others. Use the session to discuss wider issues such as mutual respect, individual rights and shared responsibilities.

Speaking

Speaking can occur in many different forms ranging from informal to formal. The language children use will vary according to the age of their audience and their familiarity with that audience.

It is important for children to know the types of speaking behaviours appropriate in the classroom, e.g. that the style of language acceptable for a class discussion differs from the style used with peers in the playground. At times it will be necessary to talk with children about the type of language appropriate for particular audiences and situations. In this way they will become aware of their responsibilities as speakers and will begin to practise and display more appropriate speaking behaviours in the classroom.

Observe and record speaking behaviours over a period of time, e.g. hour, day, week. Discuss the results with the class and brainstorm a set of speaking rules. Record the rules on a chart and use as a reference during classroom activities.

When I Speak I :

- Say excuse me if the person I want to talk to is busy.
- Look at the person I'm talking to.
- Let other people join in and have a turn.
- Use the person's name when I want to ask for something ..

When I Listen I :

- Give a reply when someone says hello or asks a question.
- Look at the speaker.
- Show with my face that I'm interested in what the speaker is telling me.
- Wait until the other person is finished before speaking.

Examples of speaking and listening rules devised during a year 2 discussion.

Problem Solving

The ability to judge and use appropriate language for different situations and audiences is an important communication skill. The first strategy in this section helps children to identify and deal with social situations that arise at school. These situations then become a focus for discussion, role play and the development of effective communication skills. The second strategy suggests various approaches for helping children choose and use appropriate language and styles for different purposes and audiences. Included in the third section are activities for assisting children bridge the gap between oral and written language.

The following criteria provide a focus for observing and evaluating children's understandings of appropriate social behaviours and speech styles.

Problem Solving Social Situations

Appropriate language for particular social situations can be modelled or problem solved during group discussion. Incorporate the following ideas, or observe and identify other situations in the classroom or playground.

What would you say in this situation?

Greeting:
– If you saw a child you know from another class?
– If you saw the teacher you had last year?
– If the Principal said hello to you?

Invitation:
– If you noticed that another child wanted to join in your group?
– If you were sent to invite the Principal to your class play?
– If you were chosen to ring and invite someone to talk to the class?

Seeking Permission:
– If you wanted to borrow someone's pencil sharpener?
– If you wanted to play with something in the classroom?

Apology:
– If you called people names and upset them?
– If you went to the library to explain you had lost a book?

Formal and Informal Talk

The language children use will vary according to the age of the audience, familiarity with that audience and purpose for speaking. Initially, speech will reflect the language of parents and the home. Through interacting with other children the language of the peer group will also begin to have a significant influence on language development. In addition, the school environment demands that children interact with many adults in a range of situations, from informal to formal. Each context requires children to make choices about the most appropriate style of language for different situations.

Some children may have difficulty switching styles or may persist in using non-standard forms in more formal activities, e.g. at assembly or when greeting guests. At times it will be necessary for teachers to intervene and make children aware of a more appropriate form.

'Relaxed' Versus 'Careful' Speech

The following strategy is effective in making children aware of standard language forms. Value the children's home language at all times, while modelling standard alternatives. In this way children will develop their ability to make conscious choices about how and when to use different styles of language.

- Introduce the concept of 'formal' versus 'informal' talk by comparing the styles of language used in formal and informal situations. For example, discuss the type of language appropriate for addressing a school assembly compared with the informal language displayed when telephoning a friend. Brainstorm and list school activities that require a switch in speaking styles and group them under headings, e.g. Formal Talk, Informal Talk.
- Discuss examples of inappropriate language for each situation, e.g. *See ya,* to finish an assembly presentation. Suggest more appropriate language during group discussion, role play, or partner activities where pairs record their ideas.
- Provide experiences that allow children to practise informal and formal talking for real purposes. Ideas include:
  - talking to peers to clarify ideas or provide information

- conversing with teachers and other adults during open days, after assemblies, on school camps
- welcoming and thanking guests or visitors
- interviewing school staff or community members
- introducing assembly items

- Observe children's language during informal and formal interactions. Help children develop an awareness of more appropriate forms through modelling and group discussion.

Spoken to Written Language

A major challenge for teachers is to help children bridge the gap between spoken and written language. Children come to school from varying backgrounds and their speech reflects the language of their parents or the immediate community. Some children may display 'non-standard' forms of speech which are entirely appropriate in many contexts. While the meaning the children intend to convey is not generally lost, teachers may need to intervene to ensure children are able to choose from alternative forms when writing. The following activities help link conventional speech forms into writing.

Scribing recounts

Assist children to develop an awareness of the way they and others use language, by scribing their recounts as they tell them. This strategy draws children's attention to the way language is structured and provides an opportunity to suggest alternatives to non-standard forms. Teachers should first listen to the children's message and then model a 'written' form; for example:

Child: *We did go to the beach on Sunday and we seen lots of dolphins.*
Teacher: *Let's write your story. We need to say, 'We went to the beach on Sunday and we saw lots of dolphins.'.*

Written Activities

Monitor children's use of speech forms and select a non-standard expression that may also be evident in their writing, e.g. *I done*. Children need to realise that their spoken language is not being criticised but they are being offered a 'classroom' alternative to use in their written work.

Discuss and role play the appropriate classroom form then complete speech balloons or cloze activities that provide practice in linking oral to written conventions.

Relaxed talking

Careful thinking

Assessment

The following list is a summary of criteria for observing children's basic communication skills and use of speaking and listening conventions.

What to look for

Do the children:

- **approach people confidently?**
- **acknowledge that someone has spoken to them?**
- **establish eye contact?**
- **request attention verbally?**
- **display appropriate non-verbal behaviours?**
- **express needs and wants, e.g. request assistance, seek permission?**
- **assert themselves appropriately with peers?**
- **relay simple messages successfully?**
- **use a louder voice when required?**
- **respond appropriately in a range of social situations, e.g. greeting, asking permission, apologising?**
- **speak confidently in both informal and formal situations?**
- **modify their speaking style to suit both informal and formal situations?**
- **select 'standard' forms of speech for more formal situations?**

The continuum of indicators on pages 51–52 traces the development of knowledge of appropriate social conventions. Teachers may wish to use the indicators to assess children's control of the language of social conventions.

SOCIAL CONVENTIONS

Indicators

Social Conventions relate to the style of language and behaviour appropriate for different situations.

BEGINNING

The child needs support to use social conventions considered appropriate for the classroom.

Text Content and Organisation
The child:
- needs extensive support to initiate any language interaction
- sits/stands by the listener but does not communicate

Vocabulary and Sentence Structure
The child:
- uses simple sentences when prompted, e.g.
  I want ...
  John, can I have a turn?
- uses one-word greetings and farewells, e.g. *Hello. Bye.*
- uses single words to express appreciation, e.g. *Thanks. Ta.*

Responsiveness of Child as Speaker
The child:
- uses inappropriate behaviour to gain attention, e.g. tugs sleeve, interrupts or is unaware of accepted conventions to enter a conversation
- relies on prompts to demonstrate social conventions, e.g.
  Teacher: *Peter gave you some crayons. What should you say?*
  Child: *Thanks, Peter.*
- avoids opportunities to communicate, e.g. no speech initiated, downcast eyes, walks away
- lacks confidence to express needs or wants, e.g. doesn't ask for assistance or permission

DEVELOPING

The child begins to demonstrate appropriate language and behaviours appropriate to a range of classroom situations.

Text Content and Organisation
The child:
- initiates simple responses, e.g. *Yes. No. Thanks.*
- makes simple verbal or non-verbal requests, e.g. points or looks at items or activity.
  Can I have ...?
  Will you ...?

Vocabulary and Sentence Structure
The child:
- begins to imitate conventions modelled in class, e.g.
  Excuse me, Mrs ...
  Thank you for listening to my news.
- begins to use vocabulary that reflects classroom conventions, e.g.
  Thank you. Sorry. Excuse me.

Responsiveness of Child as Speaker
The child:
- uses a variety of verbal and non-verbal behaviours to gain attention, e.g. raises hand, *Excuse me ...*
- requires frequent prompts and practice to respond appropriately in specific social situations, e.g.
  Teacher: *Karen, what should you remember when you're doing a partner activity?*
  Karen: *Use a quiet voice.*
- needs encouragement to approach people outside class, e.g. other teachers, children with encouragement, asks for assistance or permission

CONSOLIDATING

The child demonstrates appropriate social convention in informal situations and begins to use language in more formal contexts.

Text Content and Organisation
The child:
- includes simple courtesies when communicating, e.g.
  Excuse me.
  Would you like a turn?
- adapts language to suit informal or more formal situations

Vocabulary and Sentence Structure
The child:
- integrates appropriate language with situation, e.g. during a partner activity: *Do you want to finish this part? Can I have a turn now?*
  Excuse me, Carol. You have to finish your painting.
- uses appropriate vocabulary to support or clarify the message, e.g. when greeting, asking permission, apologising

Responsiveness of Child as Speaker
The child:
- monitors and responds to other speakers using a variety of verbal and non-verbal behaviours, e.g. eye contact, appropriate volume, clarifying information, extending conversation
- is aware of social courtesies appropriate to particular situations, e.g. uses polite terms to address adults, doesn't interrupt when a peer is telling class news
- shows increasing confidence when communicating with groups outside the classroom
- shows increasing confidence in using a more formal language style, e.g. when speaking at school assembly

EXPANDING

The child independently and confidently adapts speech styles and social behaviours to suit a range of audiences and situations.

Text Content and Organisation
The child:
- uses a range of informal communication styles, e.g. with peers, adults
- uses a range of formal communication styles, e.g. when introducing a guest, speaking at assembly, participating in a debate

Vocabulary and Sentence Structure
The child:
- selects and uses appropriate vocabulary to suit informal or formal speech
- selects vocabulary to suit a range of audiences, e.g. peers, adults, guests
- confidently adapts vocabulary and style of speech to suit range of listeners in a group, e.g. peers and adults in same group

Responsiveness of Child as Speaker
The child:
- independently uses appropriate verbal and non-verbal language during formal and informal situations
- monitors and responds to language used in small group or large group situations, e.g. conversation or formal group discussion
- speaks confidently and communicates effectively with a range of audiences
- responds to the audience by adjusting volume, rate, vocabulary
- uses social courtesies confidently and automatically

SOCIAL CONVENTIONS

Indicators

BEGINNING

Responsiveness of Child as Listener
The child:

- makes little or no acknowledgment that someone has spoken
- is unaware of the process of interaction between speaker and listener
- makes responses that are non-verbal rather than verbal, e.g. when asked a question, points to the activity
- is confused when asked to respond and interact, e.g. doesn't know how to sustain a conversation, relay a message, answer a question

DEVELOPING

Responsiveness of Child as Listener
The child:

- begins to acknowledge the speaker through eye contact, spoken response
- begins to use verbal response rather than inappropriate non-verbal responses
- with support, begins to interact during a conversation, relays simple messages, answers questions

CONSOLIDATING

Responsiveness of Child as Listener
The child:

- acknowledges the speaker through eye contact, appropriate verbal responses, questions to clarify the message
- demonstrates established classroom courtesies, e.g. waits for speaker to finish talking, looks at speaker
- interacts appropriately, e.g. during conversations, discussions
- shows an interest in what has been said by commenting, questioning, etc.

EXPANDING

Responsiveness of Child as Listener
The child:

- responds confidently and appropriately in a variety of situations, e.g. listening attentively during a class meeting, interacting during small group discussions
- listens and responds to greetings, farewells, apologies, etc.
- monitors and responds effectively to more formal situations, e.g. listens and responds to arguments during a class debate
- uses highly-developed interactive behaviours in both informal and formal situations

Chapter 2:

Language and Literacy

- **Newstelling**
- **Narrative**
- **Description**

Section 1:

Newstelling

- Newstelling has an important social function in promoting participation and confidence. It helps children develop appropriate speaking and listening behaviours.
- Newstelling provides opportunities to practise oral language skills related to initiating topics, selecting and adapting information to suit the needs of the listener, and monitoring the effectiveness of a presentation.
- Newstelling develops skills in planning and presenting the main elements of recount – *when, who, where, what, why*. It also helps promote critical listening and effective questioning skills.

Newstelling is a widely used activity in most classrooms but its full potential for developing literacy-related skills is rarely exploited.

Speaking skills developed through newstelling include initiating and developing topics, constructing oral texts, and planning and making information explicit for the listener. Newstelling sessions also play an important role in developing listening comprehension and courteous listening behaviours.

The Newstelling section of the *Language and Literacy* chapter contains information, resources and activities designed to promote effective newstelling skills.

The Language of Newstelling

The classroom is a language-rich environment that promotes various kinds of talk important for social interaction, thinking and literacy development. A major challenge for teachers is the development of communication skills that help children bridge the gap between what is spoken and what is written.

Newstelling provides opportunities for a newsgiver to construct an oral text (e.g. recounting an experience) by first reflecting on and interpreting the experience before conveying the information to an audience with adequate detail in an appropriate sequence. In the role of listener, children need to listen critically for detail, relate the content of the news to their own experience and generate appropriate questions to obtain or clarify information.

Newstelling in the Classroom Context

Like other components of the language program, newstelling instruction should be planned and implemented in a systematic way. Developing this process involves several steps:

- Observing children telling news
- Selecting newstelling objectives
- Developing classroom organisation and environment to support the program
- Implementing instructional strategies
- Evaluating the program

Teacher language plays a critical role in supporting children's learning. Teachers assist children by:

- explaining the purpose of tasks
- focusing children's attention on the important aspects of tasks
- linking new concepts to children's current knowledge
- explaining and demonstrating tasks
- making comments and asking questions
- supplying feedback and helping children to problem solve
- summarising and reviewing learning
- encouraging children to ask questions
- creating opportunities for children to share and substantiate ideas
- encouraging children to monitor and reflect on their performance
- providing encouragement and reinforcement

To sustain children's motivation and maintain the instructional value of newstelling, teachers should vary the emphasis and format of the sessions throughout the year.

How Often Should We Have a News Session?

This will depend on the age and interests of the group, and the level of teaching needed to develop listening and speaking skills. Initially, closely-spaced news sessions are recommended. However, 2-3 sessions of about 20-30 minutes a week, in which there is time to provide essential modelling and training, is preferable to a brief 5-10 minutes squeezed into a daily schedule.

With older students, it is unlikely that news will have equal focus throughout the year, and the activity should be alternated with other kinds of listening and speaking activities.

Are News Sessions Always Formal?

When teachers introduce formal newstelling sessions they are helping children to plan and present information in a logical and sequenced fashion. In addition to this structured approach, teachers should also provide opportunities for informal discussion and spontaneous newstelling. A balance between formal and informal sessions helps children to practise different language styles for a range of audiences.

How Can I Include All Children?

Try these ideas:
- Partner news (see page 63)
- Circle news (see page 63)
- Rostered news. Nominate news groups and roster each group for a day of the week. This organisation gives children an opportunity to plan their topic before the news session.

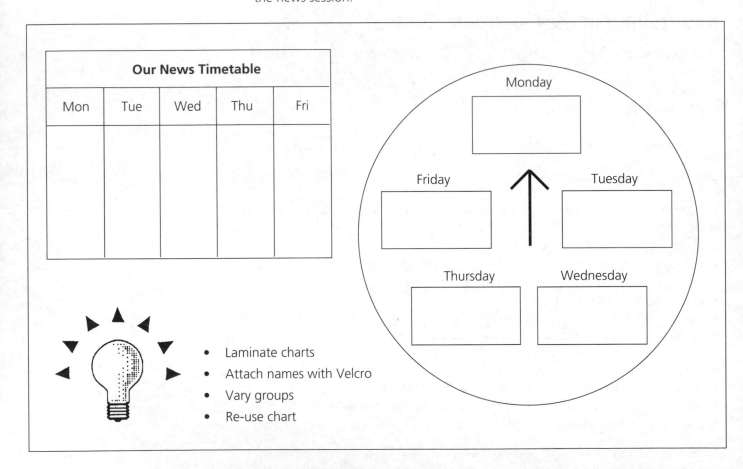

- Laminate charts
- Attach names with Velcro
- Vary groups
- Re-use chart

Newstelling has a range of successful adaptations. The following suggestions involve small-group or independent formats.

- Work with a small group of children while the rest of the class is involved in an independent activity.
- When children are familiar with partner and circle news routines, organise groups to tell news independently. Use this time to introduce or consolidate newstelling strategies with less-competent children; for example, model how to use a new writing plan.

How Can I Sustain Children's Interest?

Children are unlikely to sustain their interest and motivation if teachers always use the same newstelling format. Experiment with different formats such as:

- formal and informal news
- whole group and small group news
- pairs
- teacher news and student news
- invited newstellers

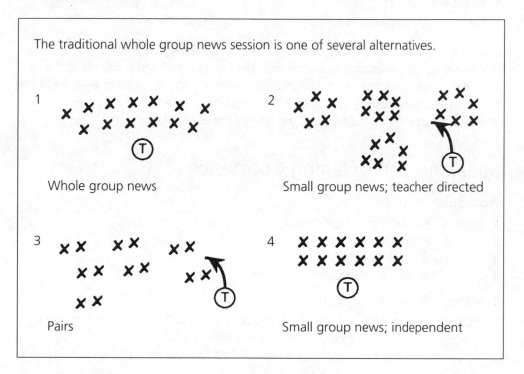

The traditional whole group news session is one of several alternatives.

1 — Whole group news

2 — Small group news; teacher directed

3 — Pairs

4 — Small group news; independent

Vary news with other oral language activities.

Partner news is often a successful alternative for reluctant speakers. It allows children to develop confidence and skills in a context that is comfortable and non-threatening. Equally effective are 'show and tell' formats where several children stand in front of the class and share one item of information about the object they have chosen.

Teaching Strategies

The strategies outlined in this section help children to learn appropriate listening and speaking behaviours, improve news content and organisation, and develop confidence and independence during newstelling.

- Establishing Speaking and Listening Courtesies
- Introducing the News Framework
- Using the News Framework
- Developing Independent Newstelling

The four newstelling strategies develop skills in a particular sequence and it is recommended that instruction begins with the first strategy and proceeds in the suggested sequence. However, factors such as the levels and needs of children in the group and current objectives in the whole language program may affect the choice of starting point for instruction and the development of each strategy.

Speaking and Listening Courtesies

Procedure

1 Brainstorm listening and speaking rules with children.
2 Record and display rules.
3 Rehearse and reinforce rules at newstime.
4 Generalise rules to other classroom times.

Examples of Teacher Support

Example 1: Brainstorm listening and speaking rules. Discuss and select those that are most appropriate for the class. Display rules on a chart.

Teacher: *What are some things to remember when you're telling news?*
Let's write our ideas then choose some rules for a class chart.

Example 2: Reinforce listening and speaking rules at newstime.

Teacher: *Before you start your news, check that everyone is following our listening rules.*
I like the way you waited until the end before you asked your question.

Example 3: Generalise listening and speaking rules.

Teacher: *John is practising the rules we talked about at newstime. We can use the same rules when we're doing maths activities.*

Ideas for Speaking and Listening Charts

Children and teacher construct these charts together.

When I speak I

- stand on my spot
- look at the class
- work out what I shall say
- speak clearly
- speak loudly

When I listen I

- look at the speaker
- keep my hands in my lap
- stay in my place
- think of questions to ask

Classroom charts—newstime rules

How well do I communicate?

- Can I be heard?
- Do I listen to others?
- Can I be understood?
- Have I put my ideas in order?
- Can I expand and develop my ideas?
- How do I sound?
- How do I look?

Am I a good listener?

- Do I like to listen to my friends when they talk to me?
- Do I try to understand what people are saying?
- Do I give the teacher my full attention?
- Do I ask questions to have speakers explain their ideas more fully?

Student self-evaluation charts

59

Introducing the News Framework

Procedure

1 Make a newstelling chart that includes *when, who, where, what, why* and *feelings*. If children have difficulty reading the key words, substitute appropriate symbols. (See illustrations below.)

2 Model how to tell news. Explain links between the information supplied and key words on the chart. Repeat the procedure a number of times until the children become skilled in identifying each element.

3 Choose children to tell news. Instruct the audience to identify elements that have been included and generate questions related to those that have been omitted. Cover key words as each is discussed.

Framework for Planning News Content

Examples of Teacher Support

Example 1:   Explaining the purpose of the chart

        Teacher: *I'm going to share some of my news today and I'm going to use this news chart to help me plan what I'll say. When we give news there are many things we need to remember to tell people. We have to tell them things like when our news happened, what happened and where it happened. If I look at these words on the chart it will help me to remember to tell you those things.*

Example 2:   Demonstrating the news framework

        Teacher: *I'm going to give you an important bit of information right at the beginning of my news. Listen to the way I start my news. Last night… (model brief news). How did my news begin?*

Student: *Last night.*
Teacher: *That's right. I told you when my news happened. If my news happened this morning how would I start my news?*
             OK, I'm going to tell you my news again, but this time I'm going to add some extra information.

Example 3:   Facilitating questioning
Teacher: *Did John tell us where his news happened? Who would like to ask him about that? Which question word do you use to find out the place where something happens? Who can think of another 'what' question to ask about the things John did at Adventure World?*

Note: This strategy will require extensive modelling. Consolidation will vary according to children's ages and language levels. With less-experienced children, teachers should be prepared to model the strategy for at least a term.

Using the News Framework

Procedure

1 Introduce and discuss the purpose of news plans.
2 Model the generation of a news plan by drawing pictures or writing notes under key words.
3 Present news. Demonstrate the use of news plans as a memory aid.
4 Have children generate own news plans and use them during their news presentations.

News Plan for a Recount

My News Plan				
When?	**Who?**	**Where?**	**What?**	**Why?**

Examples of Teacher Support

Example 1:   Explaining the purpose of the plan

Teacher: *I'm not going to say my news immediately. I'm going to get my news ready first. I'm going to think about all the things I want to say and draw some pictures to help me remember them.*

Example 2:   Modelling how to start a news plan

Teacher: *I'm going to think of some interesting words to use to describe how I felt when…*

I'm going to see if I can remember some more things to talk about for what I did.

Example 3:   Explaining how to complete a news plan

Teacher: *I'm not going to write the whole sentence on my plan. I'm just going to put some words to remind me what to say.*

Example 4:   Explaining how to use a plan when presenting

Teacher: *Have a quick look at your plan before you tell us your news just to remind you. Are you ready? Put your plan down on the table.*

Example of Year One News Plan

My News Plan				
When?	**Who?**	**Where?**	**What?**	**Why?**

Developing Independent Newstelling

Partner News

Allocate, or allow children to choose, partners. Establish a routine:

i Choose who will go first.
ii Tell your news.
iii Think of a question (partner).
iv Thank your partner for sharing with you today.

Examples of Teacher Support

Example 1: Helping children to organise themselves
Teacher: *Turn your chairs so that you face the other person.*
How are you going to choose who has the first turn?
When the other person has finished her/his news think
of two good questions to ask.

Example 2: Demonstrating and reinforcing successful news sessions
Teacher: *Peter and Melissa did a great job at partner news today.*
I'm going to put these chairs out the front so that we
can watch how they gave their partner news.
I like the way Peter reminded Melissa to ask him a
question.

Example 3: Facilitating problem solving
Teacher: *One of the things that I noticed in some pairs was that*
one of the people talked for a long time. That didn't
leave much time for the other person to tell news. How
can we solve that problem? What could you say to the
other person?

Example 4: Encouraging listeners to reflect on the news presentation
Teacher: *Tell us why your group chose to share Matthew's news*
today.
Wendy talked about a place that few people have visited
and we don't know much about it. Is that why you
chose to share her news?

The generation of a news plan before partner news can be used to help children's transition to independent newstelling.

Circle News

Organise groups of four to six children. Establish a routine:

i Find out who has news (group leader).
ii Listen to the person's news.
iii Ask for questions (group leader).
iv Choose one news item from the group to be shared with the whole class.

Kindergarten Children

Kindergarten children need a safe, non-threatening environment and considerable support to share their experiences with others. Rather than introduce formal newstelling sessions teachers should provide support through sensitive questions and comments. This approach will encourage children to share experiences with others and prepare them for more formal newstelling in junior primary classrooms.

The following activities are adaptations of 'Show and Tell' and 'Recount' news formats.

Sharing After Activities
Introduce a routine in which children answer questions or comment on classroom activities. For example, talk about cooking, art and crafts, or construction sessions.

News Pictures
Have children draw or paint their news. Conduct individual conferences where teachers or parents add a sentence about the experience. Use the news framework to structure questions to gain relevant information.

'Show and Tell' Table
Roster children to display items brought from home. Allocate a discussion time or allow partners to visit the 'show and tell' table.

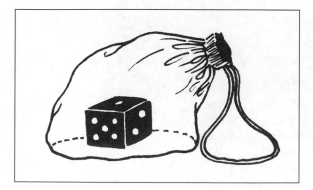

Mystery Bag
Provide a selection of items of different sizes, shapes, colours and textures. Select a child to place an item in the 'mystery bag'. Model how to ask questions to elicit enough information to identify the object. Involve the children in questioning or giving clues.

Middle and Upper Primary Children

At this level, adaptations of the basic newstelling format are extremely diverse. Variations can be introduced by changing the format and type of presentation or by introducing new demands for listeners and speakers.

Talks Based on Topics

Have children prepare a talk on a topic related to their personal experience, e.g. my pet, a special holiday etc.

Community News

As children increase their general knowledge of events beyond their own experiences, news should become more community and research-based. For example, ask children to collect and report news from different classes or school members, or report events from sources such as TV or radio.

Activity-based Sharing Across the Curriculum

Have students give an oral report on a project or activity they have completed in different curriculum areas, e.g. maths, social studies. Incorporate oral reporting as a regular feature of learning centre activities.

Developing Speaking and Listening Roles

Encouraging Reflection

One of the characteristics of successful learning is the ability to reflect upon and evaluate experiences. Teachers can encourage reflective learning during newstelling through sensitive questioning.

What was the best or most difficult thing about the experience you described?
Would you do the same things next time?
What's your opinion now, about …?

Presenting to Different Audiences

Presenting news or oral reports to different audiences helps develop children's awareness of the language styles required for both formal and informal speaking.

Using News to Entertain

Instruct children to choose a favourite news story and develop it into a 'tall story' by exaggerating the content. Initially, teachers may need to model how to create an entertaining storyline.

Developing the Audience Role

Encourage older children to be reflective, to think beyond the literal information supplied in the news, and to draw links between the speaker's and their own experience, e.g.

Share similar experience…
Share an opposite experience…
What was your reaction when..?
What is your opinion about..?
What do you think you might have done when..?

Linking Oral and Written Forms

Newstelling provides strategies to develop social, oral and literacy-related skills in the areas of Recount and Description. Adaptations of the basic newstelling format are extremely diverse and are easily adapted to all forms of oral text across the curriculum.

Forms of Text

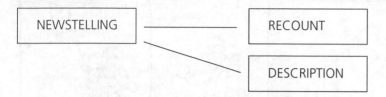

Generating Writing from the News Plan

The News Plan featured on page 61 helps children make the links between what is spoken and what is written. *It is essential that introduction of the News Plan be accompanied by modelled writing sessions where children see the transition of a plan into a completed text.* This modelling may need to be extended for children who are confused or uncertain about the purpose of a plan or the difference between a plan and product.

Modelling should reinforce the following points:

- Notes and sketches are only memory aids. They should be done quickly and do not need to be the child's neatest work.
- As much specific information as possible should be brainstormed under each key word. Later, this can be used to convey more information and create longer, more interesting sentences.
- Key words are used on the plan but not in the final written piece.

when	who	where	what	why
on Tues day	miranda I	at home	slater bug cater pilla gave it belinda	because she wanted it

Key words aid writing

Beginning Writers

For poor or beginning writers who need a scribe, write the news sentence directly onto the News Plan in the manner of string writing. The sentence frame functions as a model for early writing.

when	who	where	what	why

Yesterday my dad and I went to the park to play because I have a kite.

Planning for writing

Independent Writers

Encourage more competent writers to reflect upon and develop news content through individual and group conferences, or word study activities.

Use questioning techniques to encourage children to fill gaps in information and provide further detail.

- *'Where did your news story happen?'*
- *'You told me what day your news happened. Was it in the morning or afternoon?'*
- *'Tell me some more things about the place you visited. What are some other interesting words you could use to describe how you felt?'*

Modelled Writing and Group Conferences

Write a short text or invite children to provide a piece of writing. Add key words to the top and provide each child with a copy. Ask children to find and underline information related to key word.

Discuss the following:

- Missing information
- Information that needs to go in a different order
- Information that could be extended
- More precise or interesting vocabulary that could be substituted in the sentence

Word Study Activities

Assist children to develop their vocabulary during newstelling. Talk about alternative words that link to each category in the news framework. Brainstorm alternative vocabulary and make class charts.

Add some 'WHEN' words

Before school   During lunchtime
At night
After school
Recently   Soon
In the morning
Every week

Add some 'FEELINGS' words

Excited   thrilled
jealous
envious   tired
pleased
exhausted   angry
sad
happy   furious
surprised

Parent Involvement

Parent involvement greatly enhances children's speaking skills and their motivation to share experiences.

- Encourage sharing time at home, where adult and child each have a turn to talk about or show something from their day.
- Encourage parent volunteers to bring in an item from home to share with the group.
- Organise sharing days when visitors, such as grandparents, take part in a sharing session.

Assessment

News evaluation procedures vary according to the context in which information is gathered, the teacher's purpose for gathering information and other time and organisational constraints.

Example

February:

I WANT TO LOOK AT NEWSTELLING IN MY CLASSROOM. I NEED TO EVALUATE WHAT IS HAPPENING BEFORE I INTRODUCE NEW STRATEGIES

Consider:

1 A class profile using the indicators on pages 76–7.

June:

I HAVE IMPLEMENTED THE NEWSTELLING STRATEGIES. I WANT TO EVALUATE EACH OF MY STUDENTS NOW, AND AT THE END OF THE YEAR

Consider:

1 The indicators on pages 76–7

2 The *News Checklist* on pages 72–3

3 The *Oral Presentation Checklist* on pages 74–5

Using the Assessment Approaches

Continuum of indicators (pages 76–7)

In this approach, newstelling is presented in a continuum of development. It allows a teaching focus to be developed in a logical and coherent sequence and is suitable for individual ratings or class summaries.

News checklist (pages 72–3)

The News Checklist organises observations into three areas:

1 News content, i.e. *the topic chosen for news, its sequence and the expression of ideas related to the topic*

2 Language structure, i.e. *the use of vocabulary and sentence forms to express ideas*

3 Pragmatics, i.e. *expected listening and speaking behaviours*

In this approach frequency of behaviours is recorded.

Checklist for oral presentations (pages 74–5)

This format allows teachers to evaluate more formal oral presentations such as oral reports and other prepared talks. The content area is adapted to include the sub-areas of Topic Content and Topic Organisation. This type of evaluation is more appropriate for middle and upper primary children who have had a range of experiences in planning and presenting information to a variety of audiences.

Factors to Consider When Implementing News Assessment

Choosing Children to Assess

It may be possible, in some situations, to observe and collect data on all children. If this is not practical, sampling several children in the class provides adequate information for programming purposes. The sampling should include both competent children and those who require language support. Sampling in this way provides a window into the range of language skills across a class and highlights specific goals for language development.

Frequency of Observations

It is recommended that teachers who use the evaluation checklists observe the children a number of times before assigning a rating. Teachers who are reluctant to use formal checklists will find that the organisation of each format still provides a useful framework for informal observation and ongoing evaluation of the news program.

Using Support Staff

Including another adult, such as an aide or support teacher, to supervise the news session, will release the teacher to observe and record newstelling behaviours. Audiotaping is another strategy if support is not available.

Assessment of Kindergarten Children

Formal newstelling is not usually introduced in kindergarten. Many of the areas in news evaluation, however, can be observed while children are relating experiences, sharing information about an activity, or conversing with an adult.

Using the Information

Information about newstelling can be used to monitor oral language skills and generate teaching objectives. It may also provide useful information for a school language policy.

Procedure

1 If possible observe and rate each child in the class. If this approach is not practical, sample several children with a range of language abilities.
2 Observe and record each child's behaviour.
3 Use the summary to generate class objectives.

News Checklist

Name: _____

Date: _____

Class: _____

A　　**Child as speaker**

Area	Behaviours demonstrated	Consistently	Sometimes	Never	Comment
1 News content	Varies topic				
	Selects topics of interest to group				
	Talks about own experiences				
	Talks about others' experiences				
	Introduces topic				
	Provides background information, e.g. time, place, participants				
	Provides elaboration (expands topic)				
	Maintains topic				
	Clearly indicates change of topic				
2 Language **• Sentence structure** **• Vocabulary**	Speaks fluently without false starts				
	Uses conjunctions, e.g. *and*, *then*, *because*				
	Uses more complex conjunctions, e.g. *when*, *but*, *if*, *so*, *why*				
	Uses specific vocabulary, e.g. names object, person				
	Explains unfamiliar terms to others				
	Uses reflective verbs, e.g. *think*, *know*, *remember*				
3 Pragmatics	Uses voice appropriately				
	Maintains appropriate eye contact				
	Has appropriate non-verbal behaviours, e.g. facial expressions				
	Maintains appropriate rate				
	Responds to audience on request, e.g. answers questions, elaborates				
4 Interest and motivation	Bids for a turn at newstime				
	Offers further comment about news during the day				

　© Education Department of Western Australia. Published by Rigby Heinemann

Name: _____

Date: _____

Class: _____

B   Child as audience

Area	Behaviours demonstrated	Consistently	Sometimes	Never	Comment
1 Social and listening behaviour	Listens attentively, e.g. no talking, sitting still				
	Looks at person speaking				
	Offers spontaneous comment				
	Asks and answers questions as evidence of listening				
2 Asking questions	Uses appropriate and related questions				
	Uses questions for clarification				
	Uses questions for confirmation				
	Uses questions to gain further information				
	Uses following question forms:				
	Why				
	When				
	How				
	Where				
	What				
	Who				
	Other				

73

Checklist for Oral Presentations

Name: _____

Class: _____

Date: _____

A   Child as speaker

Area	Behaviours demonstrated	Consistently	Sometimes	Never	Comment
1 Topic content	Varies topic, e.g. personal, social studies, science				
	Selects topics of interest to group				
	Talks about own experiences, e.g. my pet				
	Talks about generalised topics, e.g. mammals				
2 Topic organisation	Introduces topic and gives statement of intention, e.g. *I'm going to…*				
	Provides background information, e.g. time, place in a recount				
	Includes introduction, main points and conclusion in formal report				
	Elaborates detail				
	Maintains topic				
	Completes topic with reflective comment or concluding statement				
3 Language	Speaks fluently without false starts				
• Sentence structure	Uses conjunctions, e.g. *and, then, because*				
	Uses more complex conjunctions, e.g. *when, but, if, so, why*				
• Vocabulary	Uses specific vocabulary, e.g. clearly labels referent				
	Explains unfamiliar terms to others				
	Uses reflective verbs, e.g. *think, know, remember*				

74

Name: _____

Date: _____

Class: _____

Area	Behaviours demonstrated	Consistently	Sometimes	Never	Comment
4 Pragmatics	Uses voice appropriately				
	Maintains appropriate eye contact				
	Maintains appropriate rate				
	Responds to audience on request, e.g. answers questions, elaborates				
	Talks for an appropriate amount of time				

B Child as audience

Area	Behaviours demonstrated	Consistently	Sometimes	Never	Comment
1 Social and listening behaviour	Listens attentively, e.g. sits still				
	Looks at person speaking				
	Offers appropriate comment				
	Asks and answers questions as evidence of listening				
2 Asking questions	Uses questions for clarification				
	Uses questions for confirmation				
	Uses questions to gain further information				
	Uses following question forms:				
	When				
	Who				
	Where				
	What				
	Why				
	How				
	Other				

N E W S T E L L I N G

Indicators

BEGINNING

Needs teacher support to choose topic. May need concrete 'here and now' situation.

Text Content and Organisation
The child:

- needs extensive scaffolding—may make a simple statement, *I have a dog.* The teacher then questions or prompts to elicit further information

Vocabulary and Sentence Structure
The child:

- uses general descriptions—*The dog there ... It's big.*
- speaks in short simple sentences

Responsiveness of Child as Speaker
The child:

- is unaware that gestural, facial expression, etc. may enhance the spoken language
- is unaware of expectations of audience and situation, e.g. speaking to a group of friends in activity time is different to speaking to the class during Newstime

DEVELOPING

Uses highly restrictive range of topics— home, family.

Text Content and Organisation
The child:

- introduces topics but needs support to maintain and complete
- clearly labels referent—who, what

Vocabulary and Sentence Structure
The child:

- uses simple syntax and descriptive terms—*I got this ball for my birthday. It's big and striped.*
- uses early conjunctions—and, then, because, e.g. *We went to the zoo and we saw lots of animals and then went home because the bus was waiting.*

Responsiveness of Child as Speaker
The child:

- has outward signs of confidence; head kept high, eyes on audience, body relaxed
- uses appropriate rate and volume
- displays items appropriately
- follows Newstime routine appropriately, e.g. *Good morning girls and boys ...*
- corrects audience behaviours, e.g. *Fold your arms and listen ...*
- responds appropriately to questions. Information may be brief, e.g. *Yes, no, red, good.*

CONSOLIDATING

Extends language beyond immediate or recent past experiences. Projects into future events.

Text Content and Organisation
The child:

- consistently includes key informational components—Recount: where, when, who, what. Show and Tell: function, attributes

Vocabulary and Sentence Structure
The child:

- introduces more varied and specific vocabulary:
- * verb—reflective, e.g. *I think, I suppose ...*
- * adverbials—yesterday, last week
- * conjunctions—unless, so, if, whether
- * adjectives—large, enormous
- uses longer more complex sentences with a wider variety of conjunctions— if, unless, while

Responsiveness of Child as Speaker
The child:

- adopts general mannerisms that signal composure and confidence, e.g. sweeping eye contact with audience members
- uses appropriate rate and volume
- responds to and elaborates on other questions

EXPANDING

Talks about events, concepts, objects outside immediate experience— community news.

Text Content and Organisation
The child:

- independently produces news
- provides appropriate elaboration and detail

Vocabulary and Sentence Structure
The child:

- uses technical and specialised vocabulary
- explains terminology for others
- uses evaluative comments— interesting, exciting, terrifying

Responsiveness of Child as Speaker
The child:

- demonstrates increased awareness of audience, e.g. entertains, use of humour, etc.
- monitors audience cues, e.g. lack of interest, change topic
- qualifies responses to questions by citing evidence or logical argument

Responsiveness of Child as Listener
The child:
- is inattentive or passive or both
- interrupts with unrelated comments

Responsiveness of Child as Listener
The child:
- uses stereotypic questions for confirmation, e.g. *Did you like it? What colour was it?*
- initiates comments related to the topic
- maintains social courtesies when listening, e.g. no talking

Responsiveness of Child as Listener
The child:
- initiates questions to gain clarification or further information, e.g. *How did the farmer get all the sheep from the paddocks to the shearing shed?*

Responsiveness of Child as Listener
The child:
- monitors news and provides feedback to speaker, e.g. *You didn't tell me …*

Section 2:

Narrative

Narrative can be described as a text in which stories are told. Its basic purpose is to entertain, although in the case of recounts of experiences or historical narratives, it may also seek to inform or teach.

Imaginative narrative texts include fairy tales, mysteries, science fiction, fables, moral tales, myths and legends. Their structure usually includes:

- an orientation
- a complication

- a resolution

    – that sets the scene, introducing place, time and character
    – that shapes the plot through character and action, building upon the orientation
    – that ties ends together in a satisfying conclusion.

Narratives are produced in both oral and written contexts. Oral texts may include a series of events told as a story; for example, 'His experiences overseas made an interesting tale'. They may also include retells of traditional stories, myths or fables.

Narrative is a complex and demanding form that is mastered at different rates and to different degrees by different individuals. Children begin to develop narrative language from an early age. They fantasise, role play and practise make-believe continually. Young children also relate personal experiences. These recounts, which are the earliest form of oral narrative, have a very simple structure based on a sequence of events. Later, children begin to produce oral narratives as a product of their imagination. These attempts are more complex and involve the manipulation of story characters, plot, time order and thematic relationships.

Children who have opportunities to share oral and written stories develop effective listening and speaking skills. Through storyreading sessions they also learn about the features of written texts and how language can be used to inform or entertain. Children who have been exposed to stories, particularly traditional tales, will approach printed texts with a degree of familiarity and understanding about the story structure, language and pattern.

The Language of Narrative

Research has shown that literacy development can be promoted well before children begin formal schooling. Story telling plays an important role in supporting early literacy acquisition.

Some children come to school with a rich background in the language of literacy. They have been exposed to a variety of books, listened to stories and anecdotes, and asked questions. They have been encouraged to play imaginatively and express themselves creatively. When given pencils these children have scribbled, drawn and pretended to write. At school, they answer questions effectively, problem solve and reflect on and evaluate experiences. Their successful adaptation to formal schooling is, in many situations, a reflection of a home environment that has prepared them for the challenges of the classroom.

Other children begin school demonstrating a much wider gap between home experiences and classroom expectations in the area of literacy. In this situation, the teacher must provide a language-rich environment that guides learning and assists children to develop literacy skills. An effective program should acknowledge and respond to differences in children's abilities to respond to the language of school. It should also recognise that the ability to write successfully and make meaning as readers is closely related to children's early experiences in speaking and listening in relation to stories, songs and the language of literacy.

Children to whom English is a second language need to be given opportunities to express their creativity in talk and writing in their own language.

Children use narrative language in both literacy-related and social contexts. For example, they engage in conversational narrative in the classroom and playground by sharing personal experiences, showing off, entertaining with anecdotes, or engaging in imaginative games and role play. In class, children draw on more formal narrative skills and knowledge. For example, during modelled writing and shared book sessions, they discuss, make predictions, analyse and reproduce stories in different forms. These kinds of activities require more sophisticated narrative language and a degree of abstract thinking.

Narrative in the Classroom Context

The following contexts provide opportunities for children to explore different aspects of narrative.

- conversational narrative
- cloze and sequencing activities
- newstime
- shared book sessions
- ritualised playground games/role plays
- dictated activity-based recounts or stories
- individually-innovated texts
- home corner role play
- story retelling
- story maps
- structured drama and role-play activities
- the bookcorner
- cooperative group stories, e.g. modelled writing
- book reports

Teaching Strategies

Teachers include many activities to develop narrative language in their classrooms. The strategies described in this section offer additional resources to extend children's experiences in developing an understanding of narrative form. They are designed to be integrated, and if necessary modified, to link with existing language programs. The strategies do not focus on storytelling as a performance skill. Instead, each strategy explores a slightly different aspect of narrative, using activities that promote interaction and discussion.

Modelled Stories

This strategy is designed for kindergarten children, particularly those who have had limited contact with books and storytelling. It is a flexible procedure in which children retell a story that has been modelled by an adult, or work with the adult and a selection of props to create their own story.

The modelled story strategy also benefits older children who need additional adult assistance to develop oral language and storytelling skills.

Character Interviews

This strategy involves a form of modified group interview in which the class questions a peer who has been chosen to role play a familiar story character. This technique helps develop inferential comprehension by encouraging children to see the relationship between characters, motives and actions within a story.

Character Role plays

In this strategy, cooperative stories are created in groups and performed by two or more children under the group's direction. Initially, collections of masks are used to develop character profiles. Story scenarios are then created and acted out while the audience suggests dialogue and actions. The stories literally take shape before the children's eyes.

Story Reconstruction

This strategy is an oral version of text reconstruction, emphasising the prediction and substantiation elements of comprehension. During story reconstruction sessions children use whole group, or small group discussion, to establish the correct picture sequence of familiar or unfamiliar stories. Story reconstruction is a challenging strategy and is best used when children have had experience with a range of activities and resources that support the development of narrative skills.

Circle Stories

This strategy is another variation of cooperative story making and is particularly useful for developing critical listening and thinking skills. The technique involves children in creating a progressive story by following the storyline and making a logical addition to the previous speaker's contribution. Creating a story in this fashion demands active listening and a knowledge of narrative structure. Before attempting circle stories, teachers should provide opportunities for children to engage in some of the previous strategies.

Modelled Stories

Creating stories is a natural part of children's play. Further, the ability to construct stories and use rich and imaginative language is closely related to children's early experiences with books and story telling.

The 'Modelled Story' procedure is a 'hands-on' technique that exploits children's love of play materials. Step by step, it takes children from the point of labelling characters and actions, to telling stories in 'once upon a time' style. The strategy is designed for pre-primary children, although it also benefits older children who need further oral language experiences.

The teacher's role in developing narrative language will need to reflect children's early experiences and their responses to narrative materials. Children who begin school demonstrating a confident grasp of 'story-telling' language will benefit from adult modelling and interaction during narrative sessions. They will also respond to the adult's sophisticated story with its resource of vocabulary and ideas that can be woven into the children's own stories.

Children who begin school without having been immersed in books and storytelling, will need teacher support of a different kind. These children will require a range of experiences and resources to help them learn the conventions and language style associated with narrative texts.

The modelled story strategy involves three steps. At each stage of implementation teachers should judge the level of assistance necessary. Some children may need more extensive modelling and support before they can produce a group or individual story. The first two steps may be omitted with more experienced groups.

The following extract of interaction is from a modelled story session in a kindergarten class. It illustrates how the teacher encourages children to recreate rich, story-like language. The activity is based on a familiar story about a hungry caterpillar that turns into a butterfly. Props made by the children were used to model the story.

Teacher:	*Once upon a time there was a leaf and there were some eggs. One egg popped and out came a caterpillar. When he came out he was really hungry so he ate a carrot (smacking lips). Mmm mm, he ate that carrot and then he found an apple.*
Child:	*I'll do it now.*
	Once upon a time there was a leaf and an egg. And pop!! There's a caterpillar. Then he ate the carrot. Then he ate the apple (smacking lips). Then he ate this.
Teacher:	*What's that? Do you remember what it is? It begins with 'p'?*
Child:	*Pineapple, waterlemon, orange.*
	Then he spun the cocoon then he popped himself out.
Teacher:	*What did he pop out as, David?*
Child:	*Then he spread his wings then he flew away.*
Teacher:	*Bye bye!*

Stage One: Labelling Characters and Actions

This activity is an introduction to the Modelled Story strategy and can be omitted with more capable groups.

Procedure

Materials
Miniature doll family and furniture, or other play materials.

Steps
1 Form a story circle (5-6 children).

2 Around the circle, take turns to choose a doll or story prop. Demonstrate and describe an action; for example:

Teacher: *This is the dad. He's in the kitchen washing the dishes. He has to do it all on his own because no-one would help him today.*

Teaching Points

- Accept and reinforce children's productions as genuine 'stories'. Encourage children to see themselves as 'storytellers'.
- Follow children's 'stories' with comments, invite discussion and question for more detail, e.g. location of action, reason for action, characters' feelings.
- Facilitate vocabulary development by rephrasing non-specific or inappropriate vocabulary, e.g.

Child: *The girl's doing her hair.*

Teacher: *Mm. It's very long isn't it? It looks like Goldilocks's hair. Is she washing it or just brushing it at the moment?*

Stage Two: Creating Action Sequences

This is a lead-up activity to the Modelled Story strategy and can be omitted with more experienced groups.

Procedure

Materials

Materials described in Stage One.

Steps

1 Select a doll. Each child take turns demonstrating an action and is encouraged to make the addition to the 'story' link to the previous speaker's turn; for example:
(Child 1)... *the lady is swimming...*
(Child 2)... *the lady is drying herself with the towel...*
(Child 3)... *the lady is laying down by the pool...*

2 Continue to add to the sequence until it becomes difficult to extend the story in a logical way. When this occurs, stop and select a new character.

3 The teacher retells the story to model narrative structure.

Teaching Points

- Encourage prediction; for example:

Teacher: (commenting on lady swimming in pool) *She looks pretty tired. What's she going to do next, Kylie? You show us.*

Child: *She's getting out.*

Teacher: *And she's shivering. Look how cold she is.*

Child: *Better get the towel. There you are lady. Are you warm? No, I think she'd better go inside.*

- Elaborate details; for example:

Teacher: *What is the lady doing now?*

Child: *She's swimming in her pool.*

Teacher: *What kind of swimming? Is she doing dogpaddle like this, or just floating on her back...?*

Child: *She's doing it with her arms like this.*

Teacher: *That's called overarm when you make your arms go over like that. Who does overarm when they go swimming? What other things do you do when you go swimming?*

Stage Three: Creating Stories with Conventional Narrative Features

Procedure
Materials
Dolls and story props
Magnetic or felt board characters

Steps
1 Use props to model a simple story with conventional story features, i.e.

story beginning – 'Once there was…'
story plot – problem and resolution
story expressions – 'All of a sudden…'

Invite the children to help you create the story by demonstrating ideas with play materials.
2 Invite a child to the storyteller's spot to:
   (a) retell the story using props, or
   (b) create another story with the story props.
3 Leave the story props in an accessible part of the classroom. Observe if children are engaging in story-telling play. Invite them to share their stories with adults or other children in the room.

Teaching Points

• Respond to all attempts as valid 'stories'. Encourage children to see themselves as storytellers.
• Select more confident children for the first few turns. Less confident children benefit from the opportunity to observe the activity and work out how it operates.
• Assist less confident children by using questions, adding comments, and summarising, e.g.
  'That girl must have been very angry. What did she do next?'
• When groups are reluctant to talk, try alternative strategies, such as individual children providing only the story ending or alternating turns with another child.

Linking to Reading and Writing

Translate oral stories into written text as a way of showing children how writing can map their thoughts.

What to look for:

Do the children:
- **label characters and actions appropriately?**
- **develop a logical sequence of actions or events?**
- **use story conventions, e.g.** *introduction*?
- **use special story language, e.g.** *suddenly*?
- **use connectors to link events in the story, e.g.** *then, because, although, after that*?
- **incorporate descriptive details?**
- **make creative modifications and extensions to stories?**

Character Interviews

Story character interviews incorporate shared book and drama techniques. Like story-retelling activities, they provide an excellent window into story comprehension. They also reveal children's understanding of the relationship among characters, their motivations and subsequent actions or reactions.

The types of questions children ask when interviewing story characters are often a surprise; sometimes for their sophistication and sometimes for the gaps in comprehension that are revealed. The following questions, generated during a story character interview session with a Year 2 class, illustrate different levels of comprehension.

The *Gingerbread Man* had been presented as a shared book and the children were particularly interested in the description of the fox enticing the gingerbread man to climb on his back to cross the river. Below are two questions addressed to a child role playing the fox:

Child 1: *What would you have said if the Gingerbread Man said 'no'?*

Child 2: *Why did you let the Gingerbread Man climb onto your back?*

The first child's question shows a high level of story comprehension, inferring the 'trickster' element that is common in our storytelling culture and one that children will often encounter in their reading.

The second child has missed the key inference in the story and shows no insight into the relationship between character motives, intentions and actions. For this child, the meaning of the story is obscure.

In this particular class the *Gingerbread Man* was a familiar story that had been presented several times. Without the interviewing session, however, the teacher may have assumed that the children were understanding, simply because they were listening to the story. Without the feedback provided by interviews, story discussions or retelling sessions, there is a real danger that many children who experience comprehension problems will be overlooked, or teachers will make incorrect judgments about the 'class level' of understanding.

Story character interviews become more than just practice sessions in asking and answering questions. They also provide many opportunities to develop inferential comprehension *through* questioning. Generating questions about what we hear or read is a worthwhile comprehension 'habit' and is one of the key strategies used by successful readers.

Stage One: Character Study

Character study activities provide an introduction to the Character Interview strategy outlined in the next stage.

Procedure
Materials
Shared book—fiction

Steps
1 Conduct a shared book session.
2 Invite children to choose part of the story. Display the book at this page. Discuss the events and characters that are illustrated.
3 Choose children to role play this part of the story and involve the audience in suggesting actions or dialogue.
4 Repeat and elaborate the role play with different children.
5 Incidentally model questions to encourage children to think beyond the obvious elements of the story.

Teaching Points
- Highlight character attributes; for example:
  Teacher: *Why do you think he helped the old man?*
  Child 1:   *'Cause he didn't want to get into trouble.*
  Child 2:   *No, no, 'cause he was kind.*
  Teacher: *Were there any other things in the story that made you think he was kind?*
- Illustrate the relationship between character attributes and actions; for example:
  That's what he would say if he were an honest person. What do you think his answer would have been if he didn't really like the boy and wanted all the money for himself?
- Encourage children to think beyond the story event that is presented; for example:
  I wonder what would have happened if the boy had said … instead of …?
  The story doesn't tell us much about the man. Why do you think he became so greedy in the first place?

Stage Two: Whole Class Interview

Procedure
Materials
Shared book
Character masks or props
Interview props, e.g. microphone

Steps
1 Revise the story.
2 Introduce the terminology 'interview' and 'interviewer'. Explain the purpose of story character interviews; for example:
  We are going to ask questions about what the character did so we can understand what happened.
3 Choose one part of the story. Display the book at this page. For children who need more support, choose an event or character discussed at Stage One.
4 Select a child to roleplay one of the characters featured in this part of the story. It is usually best to choose confident, extroverted children to have the first few turns

since the interview is more successful if the interviewee is able to provide creative, expanded answers.

5 Revise question words using the news framework. (See *Newstelling* section.)

6 Brainstorm possible questions that relate to the selected part of the story. As each question is discussed and refined, the child who thought of the original question comes to the front to be an interviewer.

7 The interviewers (about five at a time, with one question each) stand in a line and take turns asking their question. A microphone prop is recommended for this part of the activity.

8 Repeat the procedure, using different parts of the story and different characters.

9 Expand each interview segment with follow-up questions and discussion.

Teaching Points

- Assist children to refine their questions; for example:

  Child: *I want to ask Red Riding Hood what happened.*

  Teacher: *Mm, it is an interesting part of the story, isn't it? We know from what the story said that the wolf talked to her in the forest and found out where she was going. What are some other things we could find out from Red Riding Hood about this part?*

  Child: *What did the wolf say to you?*

- Model curiosity; for example:

  But I don't understand why the boy tried to trick his friend. William, why did you play that trick?

- Encourage children to think of follow-up questions; for example:

  In her answer, Mandy mentioned some special magical powers. Can anyone think of a question to get her to explain them a bit more?

- Good answers generate good questions. Encourage children who are being interviewed to elaborate their answer; for example:

  I like the way you explained lots of things in your answer. That helps us think of more questions.

Stage Three: Partner Interviews

Procedure
Materials
Shared book
Character masks or other story props

Steps
1 Revise the story, if necessary.
2 Organise pairs. Instruct each pair to nominate an interviewer and story character.
3 Ask children select a part of the story on which to base the interview. The interviewer formulates three questions and the pair practises the question-answer dialogue.
4 Bring the group back together and invite pairs to perform their interviews.

Teaching Points
• Children who lack confidence and skills often use questions modelled in the whole group, rather than their own questions. For these children, the modelled questions are a useful beginning strategy. Reinforce them for participating and, when appropriate, help them construct alternative questions.
• Acknowledge original, reflective questions; for example:
Mark, that's a really interesting question about that part of the story. That's a question we could use in the next part of the story, too.
• Show children how asking questions is a way of exploring different aspects of the story. Summarise for them the kind of information they have gained through their selection; for example:
Michael was interested in finding out why the man went out to find the lost dinosaur. His questions were all about what the man was thinking. Sarah wanted to know what it was like in the jungle. They were interested in finding out about different things.

Linking to Reading and Writing

Story Character Interviews open up a world of speculation and inference going well beyond the story text. Information gained during interviews can be used for a range of writing activities

rewrite story from one character's point of view.

newspaper report.

WEEKLY NEWS SHEET

T.V. report.

Mr. Big B. Wolf
Deep Den

Mrs Red Riding Hood
c/o Grandmother's Cottage
Dense Wood.

letter exchange
– e.g. Wolf apologising to Red Riding Hood.

What to look for:

Do the children:

- formulate questions that demonstrate story comprehension?
- ask questions that extend beyond given story information?
- provide informative answers that demonstrate story comprehension and inferential reasoning?
- monitor answers and ask follow-up questions?

Character Role Plays

The 'Character Role Play' strategy focuses on the process of creating a story using a selection of characters as a starting point. During a discussion and role-play session, performers and audience create a cooperative story based on these characters. The audience, as 'director', supports the performers whose role it is to act out a story using character masks or other props.

The strategy begins with children choosing a character mask. A story is then initiated and elaborated through further discussion.

The teacher's role in this session is to assist in 'drafting' the story. Care, however, must be taken to ensure that the creative input comes from the students and that they have the challenge and responsibility for generating story ideas.

The strategy works most successfully with whole class groups since the lively, interactive session produces a larger pool of ideas than would be generated in small groups.

The following extract demonstrates children's interaction during a character role-play session in a Year 3 class. In this part of the lesson the group is planning the story:

Teacher:	*We'll have to think about a setting and a plot—a little story about what the characters could be doing. Has anyone got any ideas?*
Child:	*They could be going on a picnic.*
Teacher:	*Which ones? The policeman, the little girl, the man or the lady?*
Child:	*The little girl, the mum and the dad.*
Teacher:	*So the mum and the dad and the little girl could be on a picnic.*
Child:	*Yeah, and when they went on the picnic the little girl might go off on her own. And she walks through the bush and finds a police station and a policeman to take her home.*
Teacher:	*Right, so we've got the setting and the characters. Let's write some down before we forget. Who can think of names for the characters?*
Child:	*Mr and Mrs Briggs (giggles)*
Teacher:	*What sort of people are they? What sort of personalities do they have?*
Child:	*Nice and kind.*
Teacher:	*What is the little girl like? Remember she wanders off sometimes and gets lost.*
Child:	*She sometimes gets into mischief.*
Teacher:	*So you think she's mischievous. What sorts of things do mischievous children do?*
Child:	*They don't do as they are told.*
Teacher:	*That's an idea for how the little girl could wander off...*

During the subsequent role play, 'drafting' continues with suggestions from the audience...

Kate:	*Hello, I'm lost in the bush and I can't find my parents.*
Policeman:	*OK. I'll find you wherever you are.*
Child:	*But he won't know where to go!*
Teacher:	*Hang on. How is the policeman going to know where to find this child in the bush? She could be anywhere. What kind of information could she give to help him?*
Child:	*Like Huntingdale.*
Teacher:	*She could have named a suburb.*
Child:	*Coonawarra. That's got lots of bush.*

And later a revision of the role play...

Kate:	*Hello, Mr Policeman. This is Kate. I'm lost in the bush in Roleystone. I can't find my parents.*
Policeman:	*Well, I'll come to Roleystone and try and locate you.*
Kate:	*OK. I hope he finds the telephone box.*

Stage 1: Creating Character Profiles

Procedure

Materials

Face masks depicting a range of characters, e.g. families, people in the community, fantasy characters

Steps

1 Familiarise the children with the masks. Introduce two or three at a time and brainstorm ideas about the characters; for example:

How old might they be?
Where might they live?
What kind of family might they have?
What kind of job might they do?
What sorts of hobbies might they have?

2 Guide children's creation of character profiles so information is consistently extended. If appropriate, record and summarise children's ideas.

3 Label and display the masks or include them in a character 'bank' for story writing and drama activities.

Teaching Points

The more comprehensive and distinctive the character profiles created at this stage, the better the quality of story ideas generated. Ensure success by:

- varying the questioning to try to extend children's thinking beyond obvious information such as clothes, general appearance etc. Other aspects for discussion could include the character's history, background, mannerisms and personality traits.

- allowing more than one session for developing character profiles. In follow-up sessions summarise the information children have already brainstormed and invite them to add new ideas. This can be done as a whole group, or with small groups discussing a character and reporting their ideas to the main group.

Stage 2: Creating and Role Playing Cooperative Stories

Procedure

Materials
Masks described in Stage One (see Appendix 3 pages 209–217)

Steps

1 Select a child, or children, to start the role play. Instruct them to select a mask and describe the character.

2 As a group, generate setting details for the story; for example:
These two characters might have arranged to meet somewhere. Where do you think they could be?
What day or time of the day might it be? Is it at work or after work? Is it on the weekend or during the week?

3 Discuss a way the story could begin. Initially you may need to model a scenario, e.g. a man who visits the doctor.

4 Choose two children to role play the story for the group and involve the audience in generating ideas for what might be happening or what the characters would be saying to each other.

5 Interview the players at the end of the role play, encouraging them to reflect on the characters' actions and feelings in the story; for example:
How did you feel when…?
Why did you tell him to…?
Involve the group in generating ideas about how character attributes and feelings can be shown by actions, voice and choice of dialogue; for example:
So you felt furious when the policeman said that to you? How could you show that with your voice?

6 Select a second pair to role play the story, adding modifications or extensions.

Teaching Points

- Revise character profiles, e.g.

  Teacher: *How do you know he's a policeman?*

  Child: *'Cause he's wearing a uniform.*

  Teacher: *What jobs do you think he does? Does he work at the police station or does he drive around in a patrol car?*

- Actively involve the audience in generating the story, e.g.

  Teacher: *I like that idea, Michael. What are some other things the dad might say if he was angry?*

  John, you've got lots of ideas to choose from now.

- Assist children to develop more complex storylines, e.g.

  Teacher: *OK, so he went out of the house and down to the shops. I wonder what his sister was doing while he was away?*

- Facilitate the role play, e.g.

  Teacher: *What could the lady be doing while she's listening, to show that she doesn't believe him?*

Stage 3: Independent Role Plays

Procedure

Materials

Masks described in Stages One and Two (see Appendix 3 pages 209–217)

Steps

1 Organise groups of three. Instruct the children to select a storyteller or director and two players. Then, choose or make, two masks for the story.
2 In groups, discuss and prepare the role play.
3 Give each group an opportunity to perform. Some groups will be able to plan and present a role play in one session. Others may need extra time to plan and refine their performance.
4 Encourage the audience to question the directors or performers at the conclusion of each role play; for example:

   Why didn't the man go straight to the police when he found his watch was missing?

Teaching Points

- Encourage children to make a connection between the process involved in creating a role play and the process involved in drafting stories, for example:
  - the need to plan and discuss ideas
  - having a first run-through or 'draft'
  - making improvements with each run-through
  - getting feedback and ideas from other people
- Some groups may need guidelines to develop this process; for example:
  1 *Work out the characters*
  2 *Work out what happens in the story*
  3 *Work out what the characters would say*
  4 *Work out actions to go with the story*
- Discuss ways of getting feedback during the drafting process, e.g. taping then listening to the role play, or performing 'work in progress' for the teacher or another group

Linking to Reading and Writing

The drama technique used in the Character Role Play strategy provides many opportunities for modelling the structure of plays and scripts. Display a variety of books that contain short plays and discuss and compare how the format differs between texts.

- research a character:
  - historical
  - notorious
  - humorous
  - fictional

- write character descriptions

write a script

make comic strips

What to look for:

Do the children:

- **create detailed character descriptions?**
- **generate ideas to initiate the story?**
- **logically develop the storyline from this point, using character information?**
- **create role-play action and dialogue that match and elaborate the story?**
- **use each other to provide ideas and feedback?**
- **bring the story to a conclusion that is consistent with the character and storyline?**

Story Reconstruction

The 'Story Reconstruction' strategy is an adaption of the text reconstruction activities found in most reading programs. The strategy uses an oral language approach to develop story comprehension skills, specifically the cognitive skills needed to infer story sequences.

Complex language and thinking skills are combined to create or comprehend stories. In the classroom, children must develop an understanding of story structure and recognise how the elements of a story are linked through the relationship of characters, setting and plots.

Although many children are exposed to a range of literature and relate easily to story structure, there are others who have had few experiences with books and are unable to make links between characters and plots. It should also be noted that a background rich in literature does not always guarantee that children will comprehend every story they hear or read.

The story reconstruction strategy engages children in analysing story content and making inferential judgments. Careful selection of materials is the key to its success. Resources must be sufficiently difficult to offer a challenge and extension to children's thinking. For example, sequenced pictures based on simple routines are not as demanding as activities that require children to work out an appropriate order for a set of story illustrations. Both are valuable teaching activities but for different reasons. The first task gives practice in simple ordering. However, it does not teach children how stories work, nor does it require them to make the more complex kinds of cause-effect judgments that story comprehension requires. This second, more complex, comprehension skill is the focus of this module.

The following extract demonstrates the process of inferring an appropriate sequence during a story reconstruction session. Four Year 3 children attempted to achieve group consensus as they worked with a set of pictures.

Child 1:	*That one would go first.*
Child 2:	*And then that.*
Child 1:	*I think he's got old gum boots.*
Child 2:	*Yeah, too tight.*
Child 3:	*That one will most probably be that.*
Child 4:	*Now we think this probably will go first. Then probably this one. He's taking the gumboots off because he's been splashing through the puddles and he had a hole in his gumboots.*
Child 1:	*No, that's wrong. He's got that one on that foot and the other one on that foot.*
Child 4:	*Yeah, and then he takes his boots off.*
Child 2:	*Yeah, that one will probably go next.*
Child 4:	*Then he finds them too small. Then most probably he will…*
Chorus:	*Buy some new ones.*
Child 4:	*And this, this would be…*
Child 2:	*At the shops. And that's the end of the story. That's him going back in the puddles.*
Child 3:	*Hang on, they're not… They're not boots. We're wrong. We have to bring them back here before he gets the boots.*
Chorus:	*Yeah.*
Child 2:	*Yeah, back in front of this 'cause they're sandshoes.*

Stage 1: Reconstructing a Familiar Story

Procedure

Materials

Multiple sets of picture sequences based on fairy tales, shared book or factual texts, such as life cycles. Avoid using 'everyday' pictures, unless as a training step to provide experience in working in groups before beginning the strategy. (See Appendix 4 pages 218–221.)

Steps

1 Organise small groups with as many children as there are pictures in the sequence. Form circles and assign a number to each child.

2 Place the pictures in the middle of the circle so they can be seen by everyone.

3 The first person selects, and describes, the picture they consider to be the beginning of the story. If there is group consensus, the next person has a turn. If not, the children must discuss this part of the story and reach a joint decision.

4 Put all the pictures into a logical sequence and practise retelling the story around the circle.

5 Take turns retelling the story to the whole class with each group member relating the part that matches their picture.

Teaching Points

* Demonstrate and discuss how to conduct group discussion. Problem solve how to handle situations where there is a difference of opinion in the group; for example:
  If everyone doesn't agree with you, go around the circle and ask each person what they think. It's important to find out what everyone has to say.

* Emphasise the importance of substantiating opinion; for example:
  Tell people why you think yours is a good idea. If someone says something you don't agree with, get them to explain their idea.

* Accept alternative versions if the sequence is logical and the children can justify their decisions.

Stage 2: Reconstructing an Unfamiliar Story in Whole Group

Procedure

Materials

Sets of four to six photocopied pictures from unfamiliar story with text removed (see Appendix 4 pages 218–221).

Steps

1 Make multiple sets of the picture sequences and give one picture to each pair of children. Assign the pictures at random and ask the children to create a story to match the picture.

2 Move around the room assisting the children. Encourage pairs to think beyond the information available in the picture and imagine what might have happened before or after the illustrated event; for example:
Where do you think these people have come from?

3 Share the 'stories'. As pairs are working with incomplete story information there should be a variety of interpretations. Reinforce children's productions, whether they are simply picture descriptions, or more fully developed stories with a story introduction and problem solution storyline.

4 As a group, discuss the pictures and decide on the correct order to make a story.

5 When consensus has been reached, choose a child to retell the story. Encourage comparisons between original stories and the final version. Invite children to share how their original interpretation of the single picture changed when they were shown the complete story information.

Teaching Points

- Don't hurry the group towards consensus. Allow all children with different opinions to demonstrate the order they have chosen; for example:
  Who thinks they have worked out the story? OK Michael, you show us your order and tell us the story to go with it. Has anyone thought of a different way? OK Melissa, you go next.

- Encourage peer discussion and feedback. Insist that the children substantiate their opinion when they challenge each other's ideas; for example:
  Sarah, you said that you think that the second picture is in the wrong place. Can you explain why?

- If the group has difficulty sustaining the discussion, assist through questioning; for example:
  What pictures do you think should go first? Why?… Why can't the pictures go in this order instead of this way? What would the story be if we put the pictures in this order? Would it still make sense?… Are there any clues in the picture that might help us to decide?

Stage Three: Partner and Small Group Work

Procedure
Materials
Multiple sets of four to six pictures with text removed (see Appendix 4 pages 218–221).

Steps
Make enough multiple copies of the sequence for each child to have one picture.
1 Find a partner with a different picture and discuss which illustration would precede the other in the story. At this stage, don't share the discussion with the whole group.
2 Collect the pictures. Organise groups of three or four and give each group a complete set of pictures in random order. While the groups put the pictures into a sequence to make a story, move around the class facilitating discussion.
3 Share and discuss the stories with the whole group, by selecting a storyteller or taking turns at retelling. Accept alternative versions if they have an appropriate story logic or if the group can justify the selected sequence.

Teaching Points

- Emphasise that the task has to be a group effort and that it is important to listen to everyone's ideas; for example:
  One of the good things about working in groups is that other people might think of things that you haven't. That's why it's important to listen to other people.

- Facilitate discussion in small groups. Problem solve and demonstrate how to handle situations where there is a difference of opinion in the group; for example:
  So Ryan, you don't think it can go in this order because… What do other people in the group think?

- Incorporate a discussion or trouble shooting session at the end of the activity. Reinforce any positive group interaction that was observed and brainstorm ideas for resolving problems; for example:

Teacher:	What could you do if someone took over and wouldn't let anyone else have a go? Would you say 'Stop it!'?
Class:	No! No!
Child 1:	You have to find out what everyone thinks.
Teacher:	How would you make that happen?
Child 2:	Say, 'Everyone has to have a turn'.

Linking to Reading and Writing

Story sequencing is frequently used as the basis for many reading and writing sessions. The following activities integrated naturally with all stages of the Story Reconstruction strategy.

What to look for:

Do the children:
- **interpret picture information appropriately?**
- **infer an appropriate sequence of events for the story?**
- **actively use prediction as a comprehension strategy?**
- **substantiate their opinion by referring to details in the picture?**
- **identify miscues and provide feedback to each other?**
- **modify their interpretation in the light of new evidence?**

Circle Stories

The 'Circle Story' strategy is a variation of cooperative story-making where children create stories spontaneously or retell well-known tales. The strategy is very effective in developing critical listening and creative thinking. It also promotes recall and prediction skills since children must carefully monitor the developing story before adding a logical extension to the previous speaker's contribution. The group must also prepare for surprises, such as a storyline that has an unexpected twist, or a speaker who deliberately challenges the next person by stopping in the middle of a critical part of the story. In these situations, children must apply creative, flexible thinking to bring the story to a logical conclusion.

The teacher's role during the 'Circle Story' session is to support and monitor the production of the story, ensuring that the key elements are appropriately elaborated and ordered. For children who need a more structured approach, teachers should select stories and resources that are familiar or predictable.

This strategy is most successful when implemented with small groups. Interest and motivation are difficult to sustain in large groups when children have a lengthy wait for their turn.

Initially, groups should practise retelling familiar stories before attempting a spontaneous story.

Retelling Stories

Procedure
Materials
familiar story, story stick

Steps
1 Discuss and revise the story. Some groups may need to be 'walked through' the whole story before attempting a circle retell. Others, who don't require this level of modelling and rehearsal, can prepare for retelling through a brief discussion of characters, setting and key events.
Note: If a story is reread immediately before a retell session, the children may assume that 'word for word' recall is expected. Read the story at an earlier session to overcome this problem.
2 Explain the activity; for example:
Now we're going to make up a circle story. This can be our story stick. When the stick is handed to you, your task is to tell the next part of the story. You need to listen and think about the story carefully so that what you say joins onto what the last person said.
3 Begin storytelling.
Some children will need to be assisted with prompts and questions, but the level of teacher support should be reduced as children become familiar with the activity, and begin to monitor and provide feedback to each other.

If necessary, support retelling with supplementary materials. Sequence pictures or story maps, for example, provide effective visual cues.

Creating Stories

Procedure
Materials
story stick
story stimulus materials

Steps
1 Organise a group of eight to ten children.
2 Select a strategy for beginning the story (refer to page 99) and explain the activity; for example:
We're going to look at this beach picture and make up a story about it. There are three people in the picture who will need to be part of the story. Don't forget that what you add to the story must make sense.
3 Commence storytelling. Assist with prompts and questions. If necessary, summarise the developing story.

Teaching Points

- Assist children whenever necessary. Assistance can be provided by summarising, eliciting predictions, questioning, and expanding the child's turn; for example; *So, the boy was really angry because his older brother had said cruel things to him. Has that ever happened to you people? What did you do?... Well let's find out from Daniel what the boy in our story did.*
- Wait and see if the group can independently identify logical gaps or errors in the story before drawing these to their attention; for example: *Let me check if I understand the story. The man loses his money at the shopping centre and then he goes home and has tea? Didn't he notice that he had lost his money? Why do you think he didn't notice?*
- Encourage interesting story-like vocabulary; for example: *Jamie, that was terrific. You told it the way stories sound in books. What was that interesting word you used to describe the old man?*
- The activity works best with a mixed ability group. If children need continual teacher facilitation this slows down the activity. Group motivation is difficult to maintain and the activity becomes highly teacher-directed.

Story Variations

The formats for retelling or creating stories can be extended in many ways.

Retelling Stories

The following extension activities are suitable when children can create a circle story independently.

1 Circle Story Challenge—In this version, children monitor the developing story and challenge the speaker when key events or details are omitted, information is repeated or the added sequence doesn't link to the evolving story. However, a successful challenge requires the children to substantiate their argument.

2 Story Innovation—Innovated stories can be based on fairy tales, shared books or previous circle stories. Before beginning the retell, indicate a story adaptation, e.g.
Adding a character...   *Smarty Pants has a sensible younger brother.*
Changing a character...   *Goldilocks was not really a thief.*
Specifying ending...   *The story must show that it always pays to tell the truth.*

Creating Stories

In these variations the stories are products of the group's imagination. There are many ways of initiating a story introduction.

- Picture-starters—Provide general stimulus pictures or an illustration from an unfamiliar text. The latter choice offers children the opportunity to compare their version with the original text.
- Story Props—Stimulate creative thinking by providing a collection of interesting clothes, masks or objects.
- Character Profiles—Provide character descriptions that must be incorporated in the circle story.
- Personalised Stories—Use a child as the central character in developing a story. The nominated person must provide a time and place, then suggest a character he/she would like to meet in the story.

Linking to Reading and Writing

Circle Story sessions provide an effective link to reading and writing. By modelling story writing with children teachers can present the language and patterns of narrative in a different medium, and provide an opportunity to discuss and reflect on any interesting story features produced during the oral activity. As well, the class can compile and compare a variety of texts by making a set of Big Books or group stories. Establishing a learning cycle that moves from speaking, through writing and into reading is a powerful strategy for reinforcing the elements of story structure.

What to look for:

Do the children:
- **generate story ideas independently?**
- **quickly add to the story with minimal teacher support so that the story has continuity?**
- **retell the story, including key events and important details?**
- **logically extend the story when they have a turn?**
- **challenge the speaker when their contribution ignores important information from an earlier part of the story?**
- **creatively extend the story when they have a turn, e.g. twists, novel resolutions?**
- **use story-like vocabulary and expression?**

Assessment

To think about narrative production or comprehension as simple performance skills is to underestimate the complex cognitive skills involved. Story production requires a generalised knowledge of narrative structure and the ability to create logical story segments. Story retelling is not simply a recall activity. It reveals children's strengths and weaknesses in handling narrative comprehension.

Developing any oral language skill requires a reflective teaching approach. It involves skilful observation of children's performance, and sensitive structuring and support based on these observations. Monitoring and evaluation are integral and ongoing aspects of teaching. The criteria for each strategy in the 'What to look for' lists assist in this process.

For more formal evaluation, the checklist on page 102 summarises the basic knowledge and skills required for successful participation in narrative activities.

The continuum of indicators on pages 103–4 traces the development of narrative skills. Teachers may wish to use the indicators to assess children's control of the language of narratives.

Narrative Checklist

Name: _____

Class: _____

Date: _____

Narrative Structure and Content

☐ Simple listing of items or events   *or*   ☐ Problem-solving storyline

☐ Basic storyline featuring highly predictable, stereotyped events   *or*   ☐ Original imaginative story ideas incorporated in storyline and narration

☐ Limited orientation provided for audience, e.g. character names only   *or*   ☐ Character, time and place orientation provided throughout the story

☐ Relationships between characters and story events not developed   *or*   ☐ Explicit linking of character attributes and motivations with story events

Narrative Style and Conventions

☐ Story beginnings and endings not marked   *or*   ☐ Conventional story beginning and ending included

☐ Ordinary conversational vocabulary   *or*   ☐ Distinctive, story-like vocabulary, e.g. *all of a sudden*

☐ Simple connectors   *or*   ☐ Varied connector use, e.g. *until, whether, whenever, since*

☐ Story related using ordinary conversational voice   *or*   ☐ Exaggerated intonation and emphasis used to add interest to story telling

Narrative Comprehension

☐ Minimal response registered to story   *or*   ☐ High level of involvement as listener. Offers predictions and evaluative comments

☐ Limited personal experience or general knowledge in relation to story content or theme can be elicitied   *or*   ☐ Offers personal experiences and knowledge in relation to story content or theme

☐ Difficulties in comprehending the story reflected in response to questions and story retelling   *or*   ☐ Grasp of key story inferences reflected in responses to questions and story retelling

N A R R A T I V E

BEGINNING

When telling a story the child focuses on concrete objects and actions. There is little organisation or sequencing. Simple words and short phrases are used.

Text Content and Organisation
The child:

- offers a list of items or actions, e.g. *He had a cat. And a house. And he gave the dog a bone.*
- makes one word statements, e.g. *Dog. Hungry.*

Vocabulary and Sentence Structure
The child:

- makes simple statements related to concrete objects and events when retelling or creating stories, e.g. *This is the goat. He's hungry.*
- omits conventional story beginnings and endings, such as, *Once upon a time ...*
- uses simple conjunctions to link events, e.g. *And then ...*

DEVELOPING

The child relates a series of events and requires listener support through prompts and questions.

Text Content and Organisation
The child:

- relates a series of events that have the beginnings of narrative structure, e.g. setting, characters, problem ending, e.g. *Peter went to the shop. He got chips. I like chips.*
- begins to integrate the sequence of events in correct order

Vocabulary and Sentence Structure
The child:

- begins to use adjectives and adverbs to describe characters, objects and events in retells or own stories, e.g. *Once there was a big man. He wanted to build a house.*
- incorporates simple conjunctions to link ideas and events, e.g. *So next .... Because ... And suddenly ...*

CONSOLIDATING

The child tells a story that has a simple narrative structure, e.g. a problem, series of events and resolution. The text is independently produced.

Text Content and Organisation
The child:

- shows an awareness of narrative structure: setting, problem, sequence of events and concluding statement
- elaborates details to provide further information, e.g. character descriptions
- sequences events appropriately, supplying supporting detail
- begins to link character traits with reasons for behaviour, e.g. *The animals were lazy so the Little Red Hen did all the work herself.*

Vocabulary and Sentence Structure
The child:

- uses descriptive language to extend ideas or events in retells or own stories
- uses vocabulary related to narrative form, e.g. *Once upon a time ... and that was that.*
- introduces direct speech, e.g. *And the fireman shouted, 'Grab the rope! Grab the rope!'*
- introduces language to build excitement and audience reaction, e.g. *He sneaked through the door, then ... WHAM!*
- uses conjunctions to reflect story patterns, e.g. *Then on the second day ... Then on the third day ...*

EXPANDING

The child's story displays all elements of narrative structure and story-like vocabulary. Explicit language is used to make meaning clear.

Text Content and Organisation
The child:

- includes all stages of narrative: setting, problem and resolution
- provides a cohesive and coherent storyline
- shows a highly developed understanding of links between character traits and response of characters to events
- independently plans and produces oral narratives

Vocabulary and Sentence Structure
The child:

- uses distinctive story-like vocabulary
- reproduces language structures and patterns when retelling known stories
- incorporates literary structures and vocabulary when creating own stories
- includes direct speech to create tension, excitement or impact
- uses a variety of conjunctions that reflect story structure

NARRATIVE

Indicators

BEGINNING

Responsiveness of Child as Speaker
The child:
- uses conversational tone and volume with few facial expressions, intonation patterns and gestures to enhance the meaning
- shows no knowledge of sequencing to link events in retell or own story
- has little awareness of audience needs
- relies on teacher prompting or questioning to complete story

Responsiveness of Child as Listener
The child:
- shows minimal response to the story
- responds to one element rather than the relationship between characters and events
- asks questions that reflect lack of understanding
- reflects understanding of story by dwelling on one event, character, etc.
- is unable to interpret main idea of story

DEVELOPING

Responsiveness of Child as Speaker
The child:
- usually uses conversational voice but may include some intonation, stress, gesture or volume to enhance the story
- begins to be aware of, and respond to, audience needs
- begins to respond to audience reaction, e.g. speech becomes more animated when audience laughs
- needs teacher support to explain some elements of the story, e.g. character motivation

Responsiveness of Child as Listener
The child:
- begins to show an understanding of the story by commenting on the characters and events
- asks questions that show an understanding of the main idea or events
- comments on characters and their influence on events
- responds to literal questions
- provides a simple retell

CONSOLIDATING

Responsiveness of Child as Speaker
The child:
- uses expression and intonation to project characters or events
- uses facial expressions, gestures, volume, etc. to enhance the story
- incorporates literary language to create a mood and develop character traits
- responds to audience reaction, e.g. uses more animated speech, waits for laughter to subside
Indicators

Responsiveness of Child as Listener
The child:
- responds with evaluative comments, e.g. *He could have ...*
- questions to seek clarification or detail to assist comprehension of story elements
- responds to literal and inferential questions
- retells key events and elaborates on

EXPANDING

Responsiveness of Child as Speaker
The child:
- uses language to create dramatic effect and maintain characterisation, mood, interest, etc.
- uses verbal and non-verbal behaviours to enhance the story
- elaborates or summarises elements of the story in response to audience reaction
- independently plans and presents a retell or own story
- responds to questions related to plot, character motivation, moral, etc.

Responsiveness of Child as Listener
The child:
- shows a high level of involvement, e.g. offers predictions and evaluative comments
- makes links between personal experience and elements of story
- shows a broad understanding of narrative structure through comments and questions
- responses to questions show high level of understanding
- questions to clarify understanding or gain further information
- retells stories, incorporating detail and evaluative comment

Section 3:

Description

The Language of Description

Description, comparison and classification are essential processes in learning. Teachers assist children to develop these processes by focusing their attention on attributes of objects and events, by encouraging children to think about similarities and differences, and by helping children to make links between the features of an object or situation and related past experiences.

- Describing objects and events is part of the fundamental process of developing concept and category knowledge.
- The language of description allows us to report events and experiences in a more comprehensive and informative way.
- Without an appropriately-developed language of description to distinguish objects and actions, there is a potential for unclear and confusing communication.
- Description has an important role in our use of language. It adds richness and variety to oral and written texts.

Development of Descriptive Language

Descriptive language involves the use of specific noun, attribute and place vocabulary. The child who has not developed this language resource relies upon simple labelling and commenting. For example:

Labelling Only

Teacher, showing picture of butcher's shop:

Teacher:	*What is it?*
Child:	*Shop.*

Teacher:	*Where do we put the stapler?*
Child:	*There.*

Teacher:	*What was it like at the farm you visited?*
Child:	*Nice.*

Children's early attempts at describing and explaining often draw on personal experiences and associations rather than on generalised knowledge about classes of items and events. For example:

Teacher:	*What is this for?*
Child:	*We've got one of those at home. My brother cut his finger on it.*

The child often ignores important defining features.

Generalised Description Strategy

The child uses a description 'routine' that involves several highly concrete, stereotyped attributes such as colour, shape and number.

Teacher: *What does your dog look like?*
Child: *He's black.*

Teacher: *Mmm, and what else can you tell us about him?*
Child: *He's little.*

The child often ignores important defining features of items.

Specific Description

The child uses more abstract and varied criteria, such as location, attributes, or functions. Vocabulary is specific and appropriate. Listener needs are acknowledged by adding definitions and explanations. For example:

Teacher: *What does your backyard look like?*
Child: *It's got a swimming pool and a shed and it's got roses. And out the back it's got a patio. That's where the barbecue goes.*

Expanded Description

Description exceeds the maximum requirement. The child expands parts of the description by relating more detail. Ordering and linking information give the description a cohesive, text-like character. For example:

Teacher: *What's it like at your nana's place?*
Child: *She has this garage at the side of her house with a roller door. And guess what she uses for her roller door! Remote control! When she presses a special button on it the door goes up. There's another button on it that makes the door go down. But we're not allowed to use it because we might break it. Only nana.*

Contexts for Description

Description features in nearly every classroom discussion and can be incorporated into many curriculum areas, as shown in the following examples.

Junior Primary Context

Topic: 'Goldilocks'

Shared Book

Follow shared book sessions with a discussion.
Look at Goldilocks's lovely golden hair.
What did the inside of the bears' house look like?
How did Goldilocks feel when the three bears found her?
What do you think Mother Bear would say if she was describing Goldilocks to a policeman

Dress-ups and Homecorner

Introduce role plays based on family themes.
Who do you think is in Goldilocks's family? What do they look like? Are there any clothes we could use for that person?
Look at Goldilocks's dress. What has it got around the bottom to make it look nice?

Art and Craft

Make props out of plasticine.
What do you think Father Bear's slippers would look like?
You've made a bike for Baby Bear! Show us the parts of the bike... How did you make the seat?

Cooking

Make porridge during a cooking session.
What is the porridge doing now? What was it like at the beginning?
How do you think it's going to taste?
Which spoon do you think Baby Bear would use? Why?

Activity Based Maths

Introduce seriation activities based on the bear characters.
Who shall we put first? Why?
How many people in baby bear's family?
How many people in your family? Who is the oldest? The youngest?

Middle Primary Context

Living in a Harsh Environment

Social Studies

Include oral presentations based on the theme of needs and wants.
Imagine that you're a tourist visiting a very poor country where people have difficulty getting the things they need for living. Describe for us what life was like for the people you saw.

Art and Craft

Make shelters such as igloos, tents, Aboriginal desert shelters, station homesteads.
Explain to us how you made your shelter. What materials did you use, and what special things did you think about as you made it?

Science

Melt a block of ice. Discuss the change in volume and link this into a discussion of how water is stored.
How much water do you think will be in the cup when it melts? Why? Tell us about other times you've seen this happen. How long do you think it will take to melt? What will it look like in ten minutes, in half an hour, in an hour?

Maths

Reinforce space concepts in model building activities:
What shapes did you use when you drew a plan of your shelter?
How can you make the space inside your shelter bigger?
Where are you going to put doors and windows? Why?

Writing

Organise letter writing activities which encourage the student to reflect on how different ways of life are influenced by the environment.
Pretend you are a scientist in Antarctica.
Write a letter home to your family describing your life-style. You might like to talk about your work, how you get around, the clothes you wear, how you spend your spare time.

Shared Book

Select shared books which show an environment from another region.
What things did you notice about the place where the story was set? How was it the same or different from where we live?

Teaching Strategies

Barrier Games

Barrier games are simple procedures based on giving and receiving instructions. Basically, they require children to interact and use language to complete a task. Children develop a range of language skills depending on the complexity of the game. Speakers learn the importance of giving explicit and complete information to listeners. Listeners learn the importance of monitoring information and using questions to clarify or gain further information. Vocabulary related to the language of description is also developed; for example, children begin to use a variety of nouns, attributes and location words.

Barrier games are easy to produce using a wide variety of formats and materials. They are suitable for all ages and abilities. See Appendix 5 beginning on page 222 for some barrier games resources.

Sources of materials for making barrier games

- wrapping paper
- magazines
- posters
- maps
- colouring books
- reading materials
- blocks
- beads
- farm animals
- dinosaurs
- Lego/Duplo people
- cars

Types of Barrier Games
There are eight basic games.

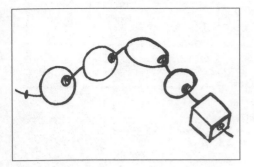

Simple Sequence or Pattern Making
Describe successive items in an array or sequence such as bead threading or a clothes-line.

Matching Pairs
Take turns describing objects or pictures. One player describes an item until the other locates and displays its matching pair. Repeat the process until all items are paired.

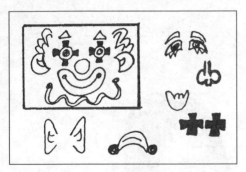

Assembly
Assemble pictures or objects from a choice of component parts; for example, making a clown's face.

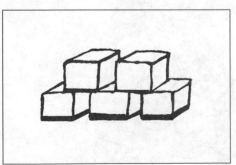

Construction
Describe the steps in building a particular construction; for example, a block construction.

Location
Choose and place items in relation to each other on a picture board. More complicated versions of this type of barrier game need careful scanning and placement.

Grids
Describe the position of marker objects on a picture grid; for example, attribute blocks on 3 x 3 grid. Older children can use local road maps.

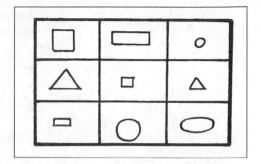

Route finding
Describe how to get from one point on a map to a specified location. The listener draws the route on the corresponding map.

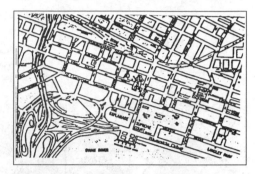

Spotting Differences
Give pairs of children pictures that have slightly different details. The children describe their pictures to each other and identify the differences.

Stage One: Giving and Following Instructions

1 Choose a simple activity, such as bead threading or block building. Form a circle with six or seven children.

2 Introduce the task: *This is a special telling and listening game. We're going to make a necklace with these beads. I'm going to tell you which beads to put on your necklace to make it exactly like mine. You have to listen very carefully so you choose the right ones.*

3 Model instructions as you thread the beads. For example, *Put the small, round bead next.*

4 As the task progresses, choose children to match their necklaces with that of the teacher. You may need to teach impulsive children a strategy for checking, such as putting their finger on each item in the sequence and saying its name.

5 When children are consistently following instructions, repeat the procedure with a barrier placed between you and the child. Give each instruction twice. After the first instruction direct children to check their necklace with the person's sitting next to them and to change their bead if necessary. Use the second instruction as a final check. At the end of the game, remove the barrier and check as a whole group.

As children become more familiar with the task, allow confident children to take on the role of instructor.

Teaching Points

Discuss the importance of following and checking instructions:

- Be ready for the instruction
- Wait until the end of the instruction before acting
- Think and say the instruction in your head before acting
- Check thoroughly

Stage Two: Teaching the Procedure

(a) Preparing to play

Choose a simple barrier game that is suitable for demonstrating the procedure. Sequence or assembly type games are probably best at kindergarten level. Introduce the game, making sure that children are familiar with any specialised vocabulary. Choose a capable child as a partner for the modelling session in which the barrier game is set up.

Consolidate the steps by asking pairs of children to show how to set up the barrier game.

(b) Demonstrating the game

1 Explain what a barrier game is.

Teacher: *John, this is another barrier game. This time we're going to make a clown's face. I'm going to tell you what parts to use. Listen carefully to my instructions so your clown face looks exactly like mine at the end of the game. Are you ready?*

2 Include some incomplete instructions during modelling which force your partner to question for clarification. For example:

Teacher: *Put on the bow tie.*

Child: *Which one?*

Teacher: *Oh, sorry, I mean the big floppy one.*

3 Show how to check at the end of the game.

Choose other children to demonstrate the game in front of the group.

Teaching Points

Ensure that children are familiar with the game preparation:

- Seat children next to each other, facing the same way. You need to play most barrier games this way to prevent left-right confusion at the checking stage. (See illustration, page 109.)
- Place the barrier in the correct position.
- Turn all pieces face up before starting the game.

Ensure that children are familiar with the game procedure:

- Set up the game correctly
- Let your partner know when you are ready to start
- Decide quickly who will have the first turn as instructor
- Remember the 'no looking' rule
- Think about your instruction before saying it
- Ask a question if you don't understand what to do
- Let your partner know when you are ready for the next instruction

Stage Three: Supervised or Independent Games (Pairs)

Kindergarten

Since barrier games make considerable demands on self-monitoring and problem-solving skills, most kindergarten children will need an adult to monitor them and provide support while they are playing. With parent volunteers, stress the importance of not intervening too often.

Year 1

Year 1 children should be able to reach an independent level of performance. When introducing new barrier games, revise the key points introduced during Stages Two and Three. After the activity, incorporate observations into group discussion. Use this discussion to:

- reinforce positive aspects of children's performance
- problem solve observed difficulties
- draw children's attention to alternative vocabulary
- consolidate key teaching points

Game Extensions

At the Year 2 and 3 levels, children should be familiar with the game procedure and well-practised at giving and receiving instructions. If not, refer to the instructional techniques (see page 111) and evaluation ideas (see page 120).

Using More Complex Materials

To extend thinking and language skills for older students, barrier game materials must be sufficiently complex and challenging. One method of increasing the demands of the task is to choose materials that need specialised vocabulary; for example, by linking the games to specific topics or curriculum themes, or by using more detailed pictures. This method calls for the instructor to provide more information within the instruction. It also encourages the listener to remember more items of information and to scan the materials carefully and systematically.

The following barrier game rules encourage more exciting and competitive play while continuing to develop children's language and thinking skills.

Many of the game variations were devised by children when they had become familiar with the standard procedure. Encourage further variations by challenging the children to suggest different or more complicated methods of playing the games.

- Question Rule — Don't provide instructions in this game. The children must ask questions to identify items. Guessing is not permitted.
- Three Question Rule — Use the above procedure but set a limit for the number of questions. This will encourage children to plan their questions carefully.
- Tricky Instructor — Try to 'catch out' the listener by deliberately omitting information in the instruction. The listener must ask questions to clarify the instructions before deciding where to place items. Deliberately providing misleading information is not permitted.
- Tricky Listener — The listener tries to 'catch out' the instructor by deliberately not asking questions to clarify information that is incomplete or unclear. Checking at the end of the game should reveal unsuccessful instructions.
- Word Bans — Choose words to be left out of the instruction, such as colours, 'big' or 'little', 'left' or 'right'. This method encourages children to find alternative ways of communicating their message: 'large' for 'big' or 'on the same side as' instead of 'on the left'.
- Opposites — Give instructions using opposite terms such as: 'at the top' or 'at the bottom', 'dark' or 'light'. To complete the correct action, the listener must translate given information.

Note

It is very important that children whose first language is not English are sometimes able to play barrier games in their own language. Children who are struggling with the complexities of a second (or third) language need to have opportunities to demonstrate their conceptual competencies when they are not also dealing with a foreign language.

Revise Teaching Points

Discuss how to:

- Set up the game correctly
- Let your partner know when you are ready to start
- Decide quickly who will have the first turn as instructor
- Plan your instruction
- Ask your partner a question if you don't understand what to do
- Let your partner know when you are ready for the next instruction
- Check carefully

Group Barrier Games

In this variation children plan instructions together.

1   Nominate one child, or adult, who will attempt to follow the groups' instructions.
2   Divide the remainder of the class into groups of three or four children.
3   Provide each group with an illustration of a procedure; for example, the steps needed to draw a route on a map or to complete a picture (see 'Cat Activity' below).
4   Allocate one step to each group and allow several minutes for planning appropriate instructions.
5   In sequence each of the groups gives instructions so the 'illustrator' can complete the given procedure. The 'illustrator' may ask questions to clarify information. If, after several attempts, a group is unable to formulate its instructions successfully, invite other class members to contribute ideas.

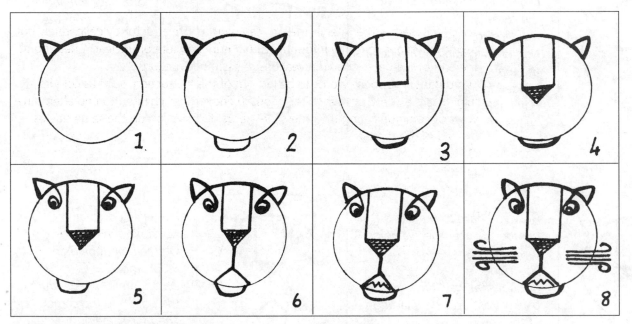

Example of a drawing procedure—'Cat Activity'

The following sample of children's language, recorded during the 'Cat activity', demonstrates how children modify instructions and become more specific as they interact and receive feedback from peers. This is similar to the drafting process in writing. Some children are even beginning to anticipate difficulties the listener will have and are providing more orientation in their instructions.

1

Draw a circle.
Shift it over a bit more to the middle.
Draw on the points at the top edges.
No! No! Draw a triangle.
Make it join onto the edges so it touches.
Do one on the other side.
They're too big!

2

Draw a semicircle down the bottom.
No, it has to join on.
It has to be so there are little bits left at the side.
It's too skinny.
It has to be longer - I don't know how to say it.
Rounder!

3

Draw a little rectangle inside the circle.
No! Up, up!
No, it has to join on the line at the top.
Longer, longer!
Halfway!
That's it!

4

You gotta have a triangle pointing down from the nose and it's gotta be coloured in.
Any colour.

5

Now you have to put a number six near the eye going this way.
No, inside!
But not that way, I mean backwards. Up a bit. Starting at the corner.
It needs to be a bit fatter.
Yeah.
Do the same on the other side.
No, back to front on the other side!
Then you just need to colour it. No, not that much.

6

Put a line down on the nose.
No, no, no, no!
On the point going down.
Stop, stop!
Do a triangle. Go down to the sides—to the corner.
Then the same on the other side.

7

Put three teeth in the triangle.
Go up like this.
Not that slanty. Make them littler.

8

Do little whiskers near the bottom edge.
Longer and then curl around.
Then two straight lines.
Then curl down the bottom.
You have to say 'Draw four whiskers on each side first.'
But the last one is different.
That needs to be curled more like the top one.

116

Pair and group barrier games are easily generated. The ideas provided in 'Types Of Barrier Games' can be applied to either context. With group barrier games, it is important that the selected activity is complex enough to ensure that group discussion is generated.

Teaching Points

- Do not try to correct children when they are planning or giving their instructions. Feedback from the listener and peers will trigger the child's self evaluation and problem solving. This is an active 'real-life' learning mode.
- Draw children's attention to those features of giving instructions that help the listener; for example, providing orientation, using specific vocabulary.
- Encourage children to reflect on their performance and work out ways of making their instructions more successful.
  After the activity, discuss successful and unsuccessful features of the instruction and brainstorm alternative instructions.
- Repeat the games to provide children with the opportunity to apply knowledge gained from their first attempt.
  Note: Allocate groups a different step in the procedure each time the game is repeated.
- Use the group organisation to reinforce cooperation and joint decision making.

Linking to Writing

Extend barrier games into reading and writing activities by encouraging children to write instructions to support the games. (See the example below.)

1 Begin with a modelled writing session that shows how instructions can be produced.

2 Allow the children to work individually, or in pairs, to generate their own set of instructions. Provide an opportunity to test the instructions on another child and make any necessary adjustments to the written draft.

3 Type the final draft and include it in the barrier game package. In addition, provide an illustration of the completed game to provide a check for other players.

Put the kite at the top of the hill.

An apple has fallen and it's in the middle of the road.

Put the boy lying down in front of the hedge.

What to look for:

- Are children's instructions appropriate: clear, specific, complete?
- How specific is the vocabulary they are using (names, locations)?
- Do they listen to instructions?
- Do they comprehend instructions?
- Do they demonstrate an awareness that communication is a two way process by asking questions, giving feedback, or changing the instruction?

What Have You Learned About Your Students' Oral Language?

Barrier Game: Checklist of Behaviours

Name: _____

Date: _____

Class: _____

Rating:	1: not evident	2: developing	3: fully adequate		
Giving Instructions					
Organises self to task; e.g. sorting materials			1	2	3
Gives appropriate instructions that are intelligible, complete, specific			1	2	3
Uses appropriate vocabulary:					
• naming			1	2	3
• attribute words			1	2	3
• location words			1	2	3
Modifies instructions spontaneously, or at the listener's request			1	2	3
Checks location of items at end of game and gives feedback to listener			1	2	3
Receiving Instructions					
Follows instructions			1	2	3
Scans and locates items efficiently			1	2	3
Asks for clarification of unclear instructions			1	2	3
Indicates when instructions have been carried out			1	2	3

© Education Department of Western Australia. Published by Rigby Heinemann

Description Activities

The following games and activities are not designed as one-off sessions. They are most effective when integrated in the classroom program to support curriculum areas, or activities and themes in the whole language program.

Classification Activities

Sorting, pattern making and grouping activities provide excellent opportunities for developing children's descriptive language.

Use a wide variety of materials, for example:

- children – their eye colour, hair type, clothes, shoes, and so forth
- 'found' objects – leaves, shells and bottle-tops
- display table items
- kitchen or general household items
- picture association cards
- attribute blocks
- theme pictures – 'food' or 'occupations'

Teacher facilitation is essential in focusing children's attention on the unique and shared characteristics of objects, and in helping them to develop and refine ways of talking about the features they observe. Teachers support children's development of descriptive language by:

Using questions
What is it for?
Where do you find it?
How is it the same as…or different from…?

Asking children to substantiate
Why did you put these over here?
Why didn't you put this one into the same group?

Modelling descriptive vocabulary
So you have made a group of narrow leaves and a group of leaves which are very thick and leathery. Let's look at the others over here.

Giving Clues

Mystery Object
Roster children to bring a mystery object from home. Encourage them to give clues, or have the group ask questions, to discover its identity.

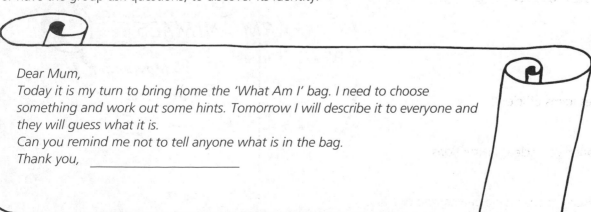

Dear Mum,
Today it is my turn to bring home the 'What Am I' bag. I need to choose something and work out some hints. Tomorrow I will describe it to everyone and they will guess what it is.
Can you remind me not to tell anyone what is in the bag.
Thank you, _____

What Am I?

Display objects or pictures. Instruct one child to choose an item and give clues, or answer questions, to help the group to guess its identity. If desired, use a description framework to guide children when they are giving clues.

What Kind Of Thing Is It?	Where Do You Keep It?	What Can It Do?	What Does It Look Like?
For example: – toy – game	For example: – at home – in your bag	For example: – fix things – write	For example: – colour – shape – size – weight

Who Am I?

Provide a selection of pictures or choose a child to be the mystery person. When describing a person, discuss with children the kinds of details that can be included such as height, hair colour, eye colour and clothing.

Description Maps

Description maps are specific frameworks used to guide the children's observation and description of an item. With Year 1 children they also provide an excellent bridge to writing. After an oral description using the framework, children produce a simple written report on the object or draw the object and label key features on the picture.

Example 1:

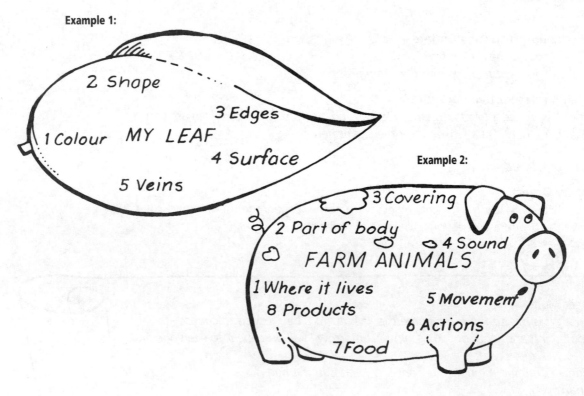

2 Shape
3 Edges
1 Colour MY LEAF
4 Surface
5 Veins

Example 2:

3 Covering
2 Part of body
FARM ANIMALS
4 Sound
1 Where it lives
8 Products
5 Movement
6 Actions
7 Food

Observation Activities

Partner Observation

Children sit facing a partner. They look at each other carefully then report back to the group on one feature they have observed about their partner. For example, *Michael's wearing a stripy green T-shirt.* This can be extended into drawing, classification or tallying activities.

Observe and Remember

A child stands while the group silently observes details about him/her. The child then leaves the room and the group brainstorms and records information; for example, curly hair, woolly cardigan, plastic buttons. When the child returns, compare recorded information and actual appearance. Encourage children to extend beyond obvious features such as eye colour or T-shirt colour and observe details such as round neckline, shirt tucked in, fringe combed back etc.

Recall Tray

Place items on a tray. Instruct children to close their eyes while you change the location of items or substitute different items. Children identify and describe these differences.

My House

This is an ideal follow-up to the 'What am I' activity. Instruct children to check a nominated item at home; for example, bedspread, curtains in bedroom, kettle, grater. Have children make a drawing and discuss similarities and differences.

Same and Different

This is a variation on the previous idea. Organise pairs and nominate one item that the children must describe to each other; for example, lunch-box, bag, pencil case, shoes. The pair report back one feature that is the same and one that is different.

Picture Talks

Before a picture talk, give the children one or two minutes to look at the picture and share with a partner all the things they noticed. 'Busy' pictures featuring a high level of detail are best for this activity.

Collections

Instruct children to find an object in the room that conforms to a particular criterion, such as *Find me something that has corners.* The children collect items, put them inside a hoop in the middle of the circle and discuss them.

Mural

As a group, construct a mural that has a variety of contrasting locations; for example, 'Bears' Forest.' Children complete a picture of themselves or a story character. Attach removable adhesive patches to the pictures so they can be placed on the mural. Each day give children turns at choosing a new location for their picture and describing it, for example:

Teacher: *Where are you …?*
Child: *Inside Creepy cave. It's dark and scary …*

Look and Locate

Instruct two children to leave the room while another child hides a puppet. Discuss the location of the puppet and decide a general clue for the pair when they are brought back into the room; for example, *The puppet is on something.* Instruct the children to watch as the pair search for the puppet. When they find it, list all the places that were checked.

Story Discussion

Encourage children to reflect on a story; for example, *What was something in the story that was … green, funny, long, dangerous, …? Who can describe the fattest animal?*

Same and Different

Organise children into pairs and nominate a familiar item or routine for sharing; for example, my pencil case, my house, what I do when I get home from school. Allow a couple of minutes to exchange information, then ask each pair to report on one feature that is the same and one that is different about their item or experience. Ban obvious features such as colour.

Listing Facts

Organise the children into pairs. Instruct each pair to select an item in the room and list five things known about it such as location, function, mechanism, materials, and so forth. Combine pairs in groups of four to share lists and brainstorm further items of information.

This basic idea has many adaptations. Fact lists can be generated about objects collected during nature walks, things observed during excursions, or investigations made during maths or science activities.

1 *They have four corners.*
2 *They have four sides.*
3 *All the sides are the same length.*
4 *When you join two squares together you get a rectangle!*
5 *If you cut a square in half down the middle, you get two rectangles!*

Giving Instructions

Art and Craft

When demonstrating art and craft activities encourage children to have input; for example, *What kind of pattern shall I make this time?*

'Bossy Boots'

Choose a child to use a puppet to role play the Bossy Boots character. Activities may include placing items on a clothes-line, bookshelf or wall; for example, *Put the shorts on the end of the line! No! No! The other end! No! Hang them the other way. Not that colour peg! Use a red one!*

Pathways

Construct a mural using children's illustrations. Label the locations in the mural; for example, Creepy Cave, Rainbow Tree and so forth. Allow children to choose a place they would like to visit and model giving instructions for moving from one location to another; for example, *Walk over the swinging bridge. Watch out, there are some planks missing! Now go along the path until you get to the Rainbow Tree.*

Grandma Game

Set up role play with two adults (the grandmother, and mother or father) and the child. The mother or father sends the child to grandma's with a message such as *I want to make some soup. Go to Grandma's and ask her if we can have a big pot.* The child goes to Grandma's house, knocks and relays the message. Grandma replies, sometimes asking for repetition or clarification of information. The child then brings the item back to the mother or father. If desired, you can use real items as props; however, the game is also successful as pretend role play. As children become familiar with the activity, include more descriptive information in the message, and give children opportunities to roleplay the other characters; for example, *John, go and ask Grandma if I can borrow her long knitting needles because I want to make a cuddly red and blue jumper for dad's birthday.*

Lost And Found Role plays
Make two identical sets of pictures of objects with contrasting features; for example:

Umbrellas	– stripy, plain, frilly, handle with knob
Jumpers	– V-necked, thick, stretched
Bag	– long handles, cane, leather

Distribute one set of the pictures, one card per child. Provide time to examine the picture and practise describing it to a partner. Choose two children at a time to come out in front of the group and conduct a role play with a telephone. The first child rings up the 'Lost and Found' department at the school, bus station or store to report the loss. For example, *I left my umbrella on the bus. It was a stripy blue one. Do you have it there?* The second child tries to find the item from the description.

Brainstorming and Innovation

Shared book
After shared book, focus on description activities.

DESIGN YOUR OWN MEANIE
What does it eat?
Where does it sleep?
What party games does it like?

Sentence Building
Sentence-building activities can provide a focus for modelled writing. Use them to produce poems, joke sentences or funny stories.

Expanded Sentences
The boy walked through the water.
He had wet boots. (Yuk!)
Then he walked through the mud.
He had wet, muddy boots. (Yuk! Yuk!)
Then he walked through the paint.
He had wet, muddy, red boots. (Yuk! Yuk! Yuk!)

Alliteration

ADJECTIVE	NOUN	VERB	ADVERB
sleepy	snakes	slither	slowly
proud	panthers	pounce	powerfully

Describing Actions
As a group, brainstorm lists of actions or sounds associated with people, animals, or objects. Introduce interesting vocabulary and encourage children to use it during role play and drama activities.

Watch your pet. What things does your pet do? Can you copy its actions?

CAT	BUDGIE	MOUSE
yawning	flapping	scampering
creeping	squawking	peeping
stretching	pecking	nibbling
stalking	biting	sniffing

Description Activities for Older Students

This section includes a variety of activities and games to develop descriptive language. They are not designed as one-off activities but should be integrated into the classroom program to support curriculum areas or specific objectives, activities or themes in the whole language program.

Giving Clues

'What Am I' and 'Who Am I' Quizzes

This activity is useful for reviewing completed topics. Organise small groups and instruct the children to write three clues about their topics. Conduct a classroom quiz where a spokesperson from each group comes out and reads the clues. Groups record their answers and keep a tally of correct responses.

Description Jigsaw

This is a text reconstruction activity where groups devise 'What Am I?' clues for a given item or topic. Write each of the group's clues onto separate cards, shuffle them and distribute one to each child in the class. Instruct the children to read their card silently and ask for help with unknown vocabulary. The children then walk around reading their cards to each other until they have formed a group with associated clues. Each group reads its clues to the class. The class then tries to identify the topic or item.

Eyewitness Accounts

This activity is based on a modification of the old 'Chinese Whispers' game. Organise the class into groups of three or four and explain how an incident occurred; for example, fight, car accident or theft. If possible, include an illustration or diagram to support the explanation (see the 'Crossroads' picture below).

Choose a child from the first group to relay the information to the second group, a child from the second group to speak to the third group, and so on, until the information has been relayed to the last group. The final version is then compared with the teacher's original version. Extend the activity into reading or writing with television or newspaper reports.

A larger sample of the 'Crossroads' activity is included as Appendix 6 on page 231.

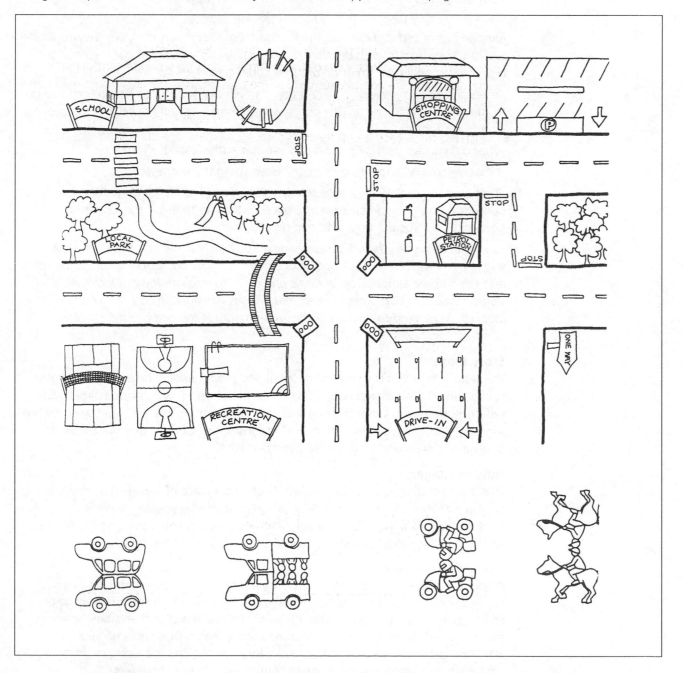

Drama and Narrative Activities

Story Innovation

In this oral cloze activity, tell or read a simple story to the class. Omit parts involving description, then invite the children to fill in these sections of the story. Use storybooks, or generate spontaneous stories using class members as the main characters.

THIEF STORY

Once there was a thief who liked stealing Voltrons. He knew that James and Kylie had some really good ones at their house. So, one night, when … he sneaked into their house. He found the toy box which was … and started taking things out and stuffing them under his jumper. He found two of James's and Kylie's favourite Voltrons. James's Voltron looked like … . Kylie's Voltron … .

Soon the jumper was … . But as he was leaving James and Kylie heard … . They jumped out of bed and ran into the lounge room. It was very dark but they could still see … . They tried to grab the thief but he was … . The thief ran out the door and disappeared down the street before they could catch him.

James and Kylie were very … . Then they had a really good idea. They decided to go to the police station and tell the police what the man looked like so that the police could look for him.

What did you say, James? … . Do you want to add anything, Kylie? … .

Is that description enough, policeman? Have you got any questions? …

The police sergeant in the police station radioed a policeman driving around in the police van. I've got a description of a thief. I want you to be on the lookout for him, he said. O.K. sergeant, go ahead and describe him … .

Later that day when the policeman had parked his car … he saw the thief. How did you know it was the right person, policeman?, … . The policeman grabbed the thief and lifted up his jumper. The Voltrons and other toys fell on the ground. Kylie's Voltron was O.K. but James noticed that his was damaged. It had … . The thief looked … . He tried to escape but the policeman was too fast this time and put handcuffs on him.

Story Cloze

This activity is an effective way of encouraging prediction and extending descriptive vocabulary. During shared book sessions cover descriptive words or passages with self-adhesive paper. Write children's suggestions on the paper and read the new text together. Variations of innovation include substitution of descriptive words with opposites, similes and exaggerated descriptions.

Guided Imagery

This drama technique involves children visualising a piece of text read by the teacher. Ensure that the children are in a relaxed and comfortable position and then ask them to close their eyes, listen to the teacher and create an image from the text. At the end of the session children share their image with a partner or the class.

Music And Imagery

Before the activity ensure that the children have their eyes closed and are in a relaxed position. Play musical excerpts and ask the children to imagine a scene or character to match the music. Share the images with the class then find a space in the room and create a 'dance' to accompany the music. Draw the children's attention to special features of the music; for example, *This is a jerky part; find some jerky things you can do with your head, arms, legs or your shoulders.*

Dramatisation

Organise pairs for a role play session. An excellent introductory session is the 'Gardener and Tree' role play in which one child is the gardener and the other is the tree. The children perform appropriate actions while the teacher describes how a gardener plants the seed, tends the seedling, stakes the tree as it is growing, clears up the dropped leaves, cuts it down, and so forth. Incorporate as much detail as possible and encourage the children to reflect this in their actions; for example, *Gardeners, be careful when you're knocking the stake into the ground. You don't want to damage the roots of the plant that are under the ground. Make sure the stake is secure and won't blow over.*
Trees, this is only a little breeze, not big gusts of wind, so it will probably only be the leaves on the ends of branches that are blowing around slightly.

This activity encourages children to explore an experience in depth. If followed by oral or written story retelling, the children's descriptions should reflect some of this richness and detail.

Listing Attributes

Listing attributes is a technique that involves the child in defining features of an item and then using this framework in a creative, thinking task.

Example A
How could we improve school desks to make them more comfortable and better working places?

Shape	Height	Legs	Top	Drawers
• rectangle	• all same height	• rectangle bits of steel	• flat white or black	• one tray
• U-shape to fit around your body	• you can adjust height to fit different size kids	• little heaters down inside to keep legs warm in winter	• barrier around sides to keep pencils from falling off • built-in computer	• one tray for pencils and one for books

Example B
Organise groups and ask each to produce details of an imaginary computer that they wish to sell. Choose two children to role play customers and choose one salesperson from each group. As each 'shop' is visited the salesperson must persuade the customers why he or she has the best computer.

Relate all its special features. For example:
• clear screen
• spelling mistake detector
• unbreakable disk drive
• high-speed printer

After visiting each group, the customers confer and choose the best computer.
The preparation stage of this role play is the most important part of the activity. The teacher may need to guide children in their brainstorming of features and introduce selling and advertising vocabulary; for example, *guarantee, discount, introductory offer.*

129

Vocabulary Building and Brainstorming

Attribute Matching

List items and matching attributes then write them onto separate cards. With partners, or the class, match the items with the correct descriptive term.

Example A:

desert	humid
beach	thick
mountain	muddy
swamp	dry
forest	rough

Example B:

as gentle as a	mouse
as brave as a	ox
as strong as an	lamb
as quiet as a	mule
as wise as an	lion
as stubborn as a	owl

Group Brainstorming

List attribute words, including less-common descriptive terms. Organise the class into small groups and read a word from the list. Instruct the children to discuss what they think the word means and suggest the name of something that the word might describe. Share and discuss the ideas generated by different groups.

velvety		
coarse	dull	neat
poor	shiny	weak
flat	stinging	powerful
glowing	murky	clear
baggy	crumbly	bursting
quiet	busy	tough
invisible	fragile	old
frozen	tall	tangled
spreading	messy	wide
floppy	strong	fine
tight	quick	burnt
light	soft	comfortable
hard	squashy	
spiky	rough	
straight		

Sentence Building

Building sentences around descriptive words can produce an enjoyable modelled writing session. For example:

ADJECTIVE	NOUN	VERB	ADVERB
fat	snakes	slither	slowly
hungry	lions	pounce	powerfully
tired	crocodiles	cruise	lazily

130

Giving adequate instructions

Older students often do not realise how difficult it can be to give adequate instructions. It is important that they learn to monitor the effect of their own instructions on other people.

- Encourage students to draw a simple picture, using standard geometrical shapes, e.g.

- A student then gives the teacher instructions to draw the picture on the blackboard, sight unseen.
- The teacher deliberately misinterprets the instructions, forcing the student to give more precise instructions.
  e.g. student says 'draw a triangle'
  The teacher draws a triangle
  The student realises that she/he needs to say 'draw an isosceles triangle with a 6 cm base parallel to the bottom of the blackboard'.

Assessment

Continual monitoring of children's performance is an integral part of the teaching process. While teaching is in progress this usually happens in an informal way. Teachers observe children, 'diagnose' difficulties they are experiencing, and modify the instruction to cater for these individual needs.

The continuum of indicators on pages 133–4 traces the development of description skills. Teachers may wish to use the indicators to assess children's control of the language of descriptions.

DESCRIPTION

Indicators

Oral descriptions tell in words how a person, place, thing or event looks, behaves or happened.

BEGINNING

The description includes simple labelling and commenting.

Text Content and Organisation
The child:
- offers a simple label, e.g. *dog*
- requires teacher support to provide further information, e.g.
  Teacher: *What do you do with it?*
  Child: *Play.*
- relates personal experience rather than general information, e.g.
  Teacher: *What's this?*
  Child: *I've got one at home.*
- ignores important defining features such as shape or function

Vocabulary and Sentence Structure
The child:
- uses basic vocabulary, e.g. *big, little, hot*
- makes simple statements, e.g. *It's red.*
- uses simple connectors, e.g. *and*

Responsiveness of Child as Speaker
The child:
- offers minimal information, relying on the listener to interpret information, e.g. *You play this.*
- needs prompts or questions to elaborate information
- ignores audience role, e.g. talks to floor
- responds to questions with unclear information, e.g.
  Teacher: *Where did you find it?*
  Child: *My brother's got one, too.*
- offers disjointed observations rather than linked information

DEVELOPING

The description contains highly concrete, stereotyped attributes, e.g. colour, shape or number.

Text Content and Organisation
The child:
- offers a number of highly stereotyped attributes, e.g. colour, size, shape, number
- needs teacher support to supply more generalised information, e.g. *What sort of things can you do with your toy car?*
- sometimes ignores important defining features, e.g. function

Vocabulary and Sentence Structure
The child:
- uses vocabulary that provides key information but little elaboration
- describes the object or event in a series of stereotyped statements, e.g. *It's a football. It's brown. It's heavy.*
- uses simple sentences that provide little elaboration
- uses simple connectors, e.g. *and, also*

Responsiveness of Child as Speaker
The child:
- provides simple, predictable information, e.g. size, colour, shape
- begins to provide more information when prompted
- responds appropriately to questions. Information may be limited, e.g. Yes. *Big. It's long.*
- shows some response to audience, e.g. holds up item, makes eye contact
- links information to provide simple but logical description

CONSOLIDATING

The description includes abstract and varied criteria, e.g. location, attributes and functions. Vocabulary is specific and appropriate.

Text Content and Organisation
The child:
- uses more abstract and varied criteria, e.g. location, attributes, function
- incorporates past experience and makes generalisations, e.g. *I've had these before and you can play lots of games with them.*
- adds definitions, explanations and elaboration to enhance the description

Vocabulary and Sentence Structure
The child:
- introduces more varied and specific vocabulary, e.g. *This is my special game. It's in this box so it doesn't get broken. You have to know the rules to play it.*
- links attributes and function in a cohesive text, e.g. describes defining features of a bicycle and adds uses
- uses longer and more varied sentences
- uses a variety of conjunctions, e.g. *so, if, unless*

Responsiveness of Child as Speaker
The child:
- modifies or extends information to suit needs of audience, e.g. adds definitions or explanations
- responds appropriately to questions, providing adequate elaboration
- responds to audience and situation by using appropriate volume, tone, eye contact etc.
- links specific information to provide a precise description

EXPANDING

The description is extended by incorporating more detail. Information is logically linked and sequenced.

Text Content and Organisation
The child:
- includes an introduction, elaborates significant features and adds a concluding statement
- sequences and links information
- incorporates detailed descriptions across the curriculum, e.g. in maths investigations, character analyses, science reports

Vocabulary and Sentence Structure
The child:
- uses varied and subject-specific vocabulary to describe significant features
- elaborates information through technical or specialised vocabulary
- uses complex sentences that link and sequence the information
- elaborates or summarises information to suit purpose and audience

Responsiveness of Child as Speaker
The child:
- provides an extended description, modifying and elaborating information to suit audiences needs
- responds to literal or inferential questions
- incorporates detailed description across the curriculum
- uses verbal and non-verbal language to maintain audience interest

D E S C R I P T I O N

Indicators

BEGINNING

Responsiveness of Child as Listener
The child:

- responds to speaker by making comments related to own experience, e.g.

  Speaker: This is a photo of Nan's flat.

  Listener: Our house is near a flat!

- interrupts with confusing comments, e.g.

  Speaker: I got this book for my birthday.

  Listener: I'm getting a bike for Christmas.

- asks stereotypic questions, e.g. Do you like it?
- asks questions about information previously supplied

DEVELOPING

Responsiveness of Child as Listener
The child:

- responds with comments or questions
- asks a range of stereotyped questions, e.g. How big is it? What colour is it?
- relates descriptions to own experiences, e.g. I've been there, too.

CONSOLIDATING

Responsiveness of Child as Listener
The child:

- makes relevant comments to demonstrate understanding, e.g. See that button at the side of the box. You can push it and the ball will roll out.
- initiates questions to clarify or gain information, e.g. Do you want me to move the red car with the black wheels or the red car with the blue wheels?
- relates description to own experiences, e.g. I've been sunburnt too. You have to use special cream or your skin will sting.

EXPANDING

Responsiveness of Child as Listener
The child:

- shows a high level of involvement, e.g. comments, questions, offers supporting information
- makes evaluative comments, e.g. I don't understand the part about the tractor. Tell me again.
- asks literal and inferential questions to gain or clarify information
- makes generalisations from information provided, e.g. If that's the only food pandas eat, they'll soon be extinct.

Chapter 3:

Language and Thinking

- Partner Work
- Inquiry
- Classification

Section 1:

Partner Work

When children work together to solve a problem or complete a task, they engage in a productive and rewarding experience. Children learn from each other and teach each other. They use language as an instrument for learning and become actively involved in a process where their language and ideas are valued and extended.

Classrooms that create cooperative learning environments assist children to take responsibility for their own learning.

- Children develop confidence in themselves as learners.
- Less confident children are motivated to interact and talk.
- Children have the opportunity to sort out their ideas first before presenting them to a wider audience.
- Children have opportunities to talk for different purposes and with a range of audiences.
- Children practise the social skills involved in cooperating and working with others.

The following question was answered by a group of children who had been involved in a variety of partner work activities.

The Language of Partner Work

Partner and group work makes complex demands on speakers and listeners. Children must use language to plan, negotiate roles, monitor the task and reflect on the outcome of the activity. The following table describes how children use language during partner work.

What Children Do	How Children Use Language	What Children Say
1 Plan	Suggest ideas Give feedback Disagree Reach consensus	*No, Let's not have trees there.* *We could get…* *Why don't we…* *Let's do…*
2 Negotiate Roles	Allocate roles Give instructions Request help Ask permission Tutor Consult Invite	*You do some drawing and I'll do some.* *Try one in there. I'll help you.* *Do you want to do some of this?*
3 Monitor the Task	Give feedback Reinforce Challenge Explain Problem solve	*Very nice.* *What are you doing?* *Is that a dinosaur or a tree?* *What sort?* *We're nearly finished — no, you've got to put all those things on.*
4 Reflect on the Task	Comment Describe Evaluate	*Sometimes it shows up really dark.* *I like the bit at the top.* *We could have used some crepe paper.*

Contexts for Partner Work

Pair and small-group work create rich and varied opportunities for social and cognitive development. During play and work children can be observed discussing, contesting opinions and exchanging views. Discussion generated by alternative points of view encourages reflection and produces important shifts in thinking. The language used initially for coordinating a joint activity becomes a tool for thinking and problem solving.

Successful participation in partner or group work demands a range of social skills such as sharing, trusting and tolerating other points of view. It also involves specific language skills needed for discussing and negotiating. To develop these important skills, the school program needs to promote partner work within a long-term plan. For example, independent group activities in middle and upper primary classes are more successful when the children have been involved in cooperative group work since their junior primary years. In addition, when junior primary teachers recognise and exploit their students' natural inclination for sharing and interaction, they are taking positive steps towards reducing many of the negative attitudes and behaviours that may develop in later years.

Although interaction through partner work provides natural conditions for learning, there are some children who need additional support to work cooperatively. Children who have difficulty working interactively are:

- children who may have limited acceptance by their peers or who are consistently excluded from the group;
- children who cause conflicts or disruptions; and
- those who prefer to work alone.

These problems may also relate to a traditional school organisation that discourages children from working together and offers little opportunity to practise cooperative skills.

The following extract of dialogue illustrates what can be achieved when partner activities are included in a kindergarten program. The dialogue demonstrates language as an active learning tool. It also highlights the value of partner work in promoting cooperation and sharing.

The activity involves children making a collage with paper cutouts of various shapes and colours.

Child 1:	*I've got a circle, a circle, a circle!*
Child 2:	*It's a circle.*
Child 3:	*You've got a circle; I've got a square. I'll put this one there and I'll put this one over it.*
Child 2:	*I'm going to put this over there.*
Child 3:	*I might put this like this. Up a bit. And I can put that there. What are you going to do with that?*
Child 2:	*Do you want one too?*
Child 3:	*Yeah!*
Child 2:	*Do you want blue or green?*
Child 3:	*Really?*
Child 2:	*Yeah, you can have it.*

The effectiveness of partner work will depend on the complexity of the task and level of cooperation required to plan and complete the activity. Suggestions for partner work activities are outlined below. They move from simple tasks that require basic levels of cooperation to more complex tasks that demand a high level of planning and negotiation.

Sharing and helping	–	involve basic levels of cooperation
Negotiating, planning, making mutual decisions, consulting	–	involve more complex levels of cooperation

Suggestions for Partner Work

- shared jobs e.g. tidying home corner
- setting up display table
- block building
- collage
- jigsaws
- making classroom sign
- pattern making
- sorting and classification activities
- labelling picture
- brainstorming and list-making
- shared drawing
- bookcorner display
- model construction
- shop games
- computer game
- maths problem solving
- science investigations
- writing thank you card or invitations
- tallies and graphs
- story writing
- library research
- sequencing activities
- mapping activities

Teaching Strategies

Four instructional stages are included in this section. Each stage introduces key skills for working cooperatively with a partner. Particular emphasis is given to the language of negotiation; for example, joint planning and seeking consensus.

Focus on Sharing and Cooperation

The strategy is the most appropriate starting point for kindergarten children. At this level, social skills are generally taught incidentally in response to teacher observation of children's behaviours. In addition, teachers should begin to focus on group discussions that relate to sharing and respecting others' rights. In some instances teachers may also need to model the types of language and behaviour that are acceptable in the classroom.

Procedure

- Observe children interacting with peers. Reinforce cooperative behaviours such as:
    sitting near the person
    sharing toys and materials
    being careful to avoid knocking other people's work
    asking to use materials or to join in
    inviting another child to have a turn
    making room for another child
    asking for help from another child
    offering to help another child
    letting someone else have the first turn
    apologising to another child
    It may be necessary to model what to do and say.
- Set up situations in which children work with a partner, such as:
    building a block construction
    making a collage picture
    completing a jigsaw puzzle
    Young children often revert to parallel play in these situations. For example, it is common to observe children building separate block constructions or dividing the page into two sections before they make a start! To promote interaction it will be necessary to redirect the partners towards a shared task.
- Observe and note situations where there is conflict. Base group discussion and role-play activities around these incidents. Puppets provide an effective way of dealing with issues without threatening or drawing attention to particular children.
- Reinforce the sharing and cooperation theme by choosing books about feelings and social relationships.

Teaching Points

- Create a positive environment of sharing and cooperation by reinforcing positive peer behaviour; for example:
    I'm so pleased today at the way people are talking together and helping each other. Just a moment ago I heard Lim say…
- Arrange for children to interact with older or younger children with whom they may be familiar or unfamiliar. Interaction with unfamiliar speakers places more challenging demands on children's language abilities.
- Encourage children to consult each other instead of adults for help and opinion. If

the teacher is always present while the children are engaged in a partner activity, most of their talk will be directed to the adult, not to each other. Independent partner work encourages self-regulation and problem-solving skills.

- Partner activities provide opportunities for teaching aggressive or immature children how to interact with peers. Some of these behaviours may call for specific training; for example:

   Yong and Maria, I want you to put away the blocks. Perhaps you should talk first and decide who's going to pack away the big blocks and who will do the little ones.

What to look for:

Do the children:

- **share materials?**
- **have strategies for joining in activities, e.g.**
  asking permission, requesting help?
- **have strategies for involving peers, e.g.**
  inviting, offering help?
- **have strategies for resolving conflicts?**

Focus on Negotiation of Roles and Tasks

This strategy focuses more closely on the skills involved in collaborating to complete a task. Much of the children's conversation at this stage is involved in regulating each other's actions; for example:

You can do some drawing and I'll do some.
You can start colouring in something else.
Do you want to do this?

At this stage the interaction is still not a 'true' collaboration; it may lack negotiation and mutual decision making. But reflected in the beginnings of interaction is a willingness to work together and share the task. In addition, children are learning to coordinate themselves and others to complete a task. This type of organisation represents a significant cognitive and social achievement.

The following criteria provide guidelines for observing basic negotiation skills.

Procedure

- Introduce the concept of cooperation by brainstorming situations in which people have to help each other to complete a task; for example:

   At school – packing away chairs, tidying up, setting up sports games, preparing art and crafts materials
   At home – doing dishes, looking after pets, helping to plan items for a holiday.
   Discuss problems that can arise in these situations and brainstorm ways of resolving them. The activity can also provide an introduction to drama or role-play sessions.

- Choose a partner activity. Before children begin the task, discuss important points to remember; for example:

   deciding where to sit
   deciding where to put materials so both people can have access
   deciding what each person is going to do
   making sure both people are having turns
   swapping so people have a turn at doing different things

checking with a partner that she/he agrees with your idea
helping each other

Role play is an enjoyable and effective way of introducing partner work activities. It also provides a clear purpose and focus for the session. It is most effective when both cooperative and uncooperative behaviours are demonstrated.

- Organise partner activities. Observe and facilitate cooperative behaviours; for example:

    John, before you begin, check with Marco about the best colour you should use.

- Bring the class together to share completed work and to reflect on the experience of working with a partner; for example:

    I noticed Leanne and Juanita talking about the materials they would use.

- Provide examples of cooperative behaviours observed in the session; for example:

    How did you and your partner do the activity?
    How did you work out who would have a turn?
    Did you have any problems? How did you sort them out?
    How would it be different doing it on your own?

Teaching Points

- When children are unfamiliar with independent, partner or group work, use partner activities that involve simple kinds of decision making. This approach reduces the potential for conflict. (A list of recommended activities is provided on page 139.)
- Initially, allow children to work with friends. However, it is also important that children are exposed to a variety of partners and learn to cope with different styles of interaction.
- Experiment with different pairings. Strong-weak combinations are not necessarily the ideal, as the stronger child will tend to dominate. In this situation, neither child will learn new skills.
- Intervene to prevent problems only when it becomes evident that the children cannot resolve a problem independently.

What to look for:

Do the children:
- **share responsibility for the task?**
- **negotiate role and actions? Do they know what's to be done and who will do what?**
- **consult with partners before proceeding with action?**
- **help each other?**
- **provide positive feedback and encouragement for partners?**

Focus on Joint Planning and Decision Making

This strategy is introduced when children can cooperate and share to complete a task. At this stage they are ready to add another dimension to partner work. With effective teacher support and facilitation, children can be introduced to more complex tasks that require joint planning and decisions. Introducing an element of consensus requires children to use language to reach a mutual understanding of:

- what the task involves
- how it can be completed

The following criteria provide guidelines for observing the social behaviours necessary for joint decisions and planning.

Procedure

- Choose partner activities that are sufficiently complex. They should require children to reach consensus about what is to be done and how it can be achieved. Tasks should be meaningful, with scope for genuine interaction.
- Introduce the concept of planning ideas together; for example:
  why it's a good idea to first plan the activity together
  how to share your ideas
  how to encourage your partner to share ideas
  listening to someone else's ideas and adding to them
- Before children collect materials, allow five minutes to sit and plan with their partner. Briefly reconvene the class and encourage children to report ideas.
- Proceed with the partner activity. Observe and facilitate cooperative behaviour.
- Stop midway through the session. Tell children the time remaining to finish the activity. Include another five minutes for planning how to finish the task. This is best done away from the area where children have been working since it allows children to move from the 'doing' mode back into the 'planning and discussion' mode.
- Allow time at the end of the activity for children to share their work with the class.
- Review the activity through group sharing and discussion; for example:
  What things did you decide when you were planning?
  Did you change your mind about anything?
  Were there any times when you couldn't agree?
  What did you do?
  How did it help working with a partner?

Brainstorm solutions to problems through group discussion or role play.

Teaching Points

- Encourage children to keep talking to their partners. The amount of talking will naturally reduce during the task as children make decisions. However, silence is often a sign that they are no longer monitoring or consulting with each other; for example:
  Oh, Hans, that looks interesting. Tell your partner what you are doing.
  Sofia, I like the way you and Melissa are talking together about the problem.
  Melissa, your partner is doing very careful printing. When she's finished, you could tell her what a good job she's done.
- Discuss the kinds of language that children can use in particular situations; for example:

Teacher: *What could you say if you listened to your partner's idea and you didn't think it would work?*

Child: *That's no good!*

Teacher: *Well, you would need to explain why, too. What if she/he wanted to colour the page in green but the title was already green? You would say, 'We can't do that because...'*

Child: *We won't be able to see the title!*

Teacher: *And perhaps you could suggest another colour to use instead. What would you say if your partner had a really good idea?*

- Resist the temptation to abandon the second planning session (fifth bullet point from top of this page) if children are busy. Monitoring and reviewing are important aspects of the planning process. This brief 'thinking' time tends to heighten rather than reduce motivation.

What to look for:

Do the children:

- **take responsibility for initiating ideas?**
- **respond to and discuss each other's ideas?**
- **challenge their partner's ideas?**
- **clarify and explain ideas?**
- **reach consensus?**
- **monitor task and check each other's performance?**
- **engage in joint problem solving?**

Focus on Wider Sharing and Consultation

This strategy encourages children to share 'work in progress' with peers by eliciting comment and feedback. When children seek an audience response they are encouraged to step back mentally from what they are doing and evaluate their own work. They also learn that peers can be an important source of ideas and support.

The following criteria provide guidelines for observing the behaviours necessary for sharing and consulting with peers.

Procedure

- Select partner activities that will encourage children to talk, ask questions, and express their ideas and opinions.
- Stop the group midway through the session. Invite children to share 'work in progress'. If questioning and discussion do not emerge spontaneously, revise the 'audience role'; for example:

    ask a question
    say one thing you like about the model
    suggest an idea for something that could be added

    Teacher modelling using an item of work may be useful; for example:
    Can you help me with this part? I'll tell you what my problem is... Thank you, Daniel, I might try using that idea.

Note: Teachers should continue with whole-group sharing until children are familiar with the procedure and discuss and offer constructive comments about each other's work.

- Replace class sharing with small-group sharing sessions where two pairs take turns to share their work. Observe and facilitate groups as necessary.
- Briefly reconvene the whole group after each session. Invite children to share any new thoughts or ideas gained from talking with others.

Teaching Points

- Reinforce the positive benefits of sharing and consulting with others; for example:
    The two pairs over there – Daniel and Nilgun and Pierre and Marta – I really liked the way you were helping by thinking of good ideas for each other.
- Facilitate an interested, positive response in the small group sharing; for example:
    Pierre and Marta had some interesting ideas for different places in their story, didn't they?
    Marco, have you asked Jade about this part of her model?

What to look for:

Do the children:

- **share and describe their work?**
- **demonstrate an interest in other people's work and ideas? For example, do they ask questions?**
- **offer constructive feedback and suggestions to each other?**
- **use ideas suggested by other people?**

Reflecting on Partner Work Skills

It is important that children are given opportunities to reflect not only on the task undertaken during partner work, but also on the strategies and outcomes of partner work.

Procedure

Before a task is undertaken… talk about goals, parameters, ways and means.

During activity… stop and talk about how consensus was reached and what form the collaboration is taking.

After the task is finished… assess not only the product, but the process.

   Was each able to contribute effectively?
   How did partners help each other if the need arose?
   How did partners deal with conflict?
   What was the best thing about it?

Teaching Points

A focus can be placed on three principles:

- Consensus

  The best way to achieve a good result is through consensus. It is a good idea to talk things through so that each person has the same understanding of the task, adopts the same goals, and shares decisions about ways and means. What are people good at? What might a person need help with?

- Collaboration

  Work is best accomplished through collaboration. Each person is working with the other, each is making a crucial contribution. The goal is reached through collaboration, not competition. How can partners judge that things are going well?

- Each worker is a winner

  When there is consensus and tasks are achieved through cooperation, then every single person wins, as the outcome is the best one for everyone and everyone has a sense of achievement.

Assessment

The development of oral language skills calls for a reflective teaching approach. It involves skilful observation of children's performance and sensitive structuring and support based on these observations. This method of diagnostic teaching is particularly important in partner work sessions.

Difficulties observed during partner work can be addressed 'on the spot' by giving individual help. They can also become the focus for group discussion and problem solving. The observational criteria in the 'What to look for' lists will assist in this process.

More formal evaluation can be carried out using the checklist below.

In addition, the continuum of indicators on pages 147–8 traces the development of partner work skills. Teachers may wish to use the indicators to assess children's control of the language of partner work.

Name: _____

Class: _____

Date: _____

Partner Work Evaluation

☐ Undertakes task separately	*or*	☐ Undertakes task cooperatively
☐ Mostly silent, particularly in latter stages of task	*or*	☐ Talk evident throughout task
☐ Dominant or passive pattern of interaction	*or*	☐ Relatively equal participation with partner
☐ Issues instructions or proceeds without checking with partner	*or*	☐ Negotiates with partner; seeks consensus
☐ Ignores partner's work or comments negatively	*or*	☐ Reinforces partner's efforts; comments positively
☐ Does not plan task	*or*	☐ Plans; discusses ideas with partner
☐ No evidence of task monitoring	*or*	☐ Evidence of task monitoring, such as: gives feedback, challenges, explains, engages in problem solving
☐ Talk only relates to immediate task	*or*	☐ Offers reflective or evaluative comments; may discuss similar tasks or experiences

PARTNER WORK

Indicators

Partner activities place an emphasis on language generated through interactive behaviour.

BEGINNING

The child needs support to initiate cooperative tasks.

Text Content and Organisation
The child:

- makes simple comments or gives direct instructions, e.g.
  It's mine. Give it to me. I'll do it. You watch.
- relies on teacher support to interact with partner

Vocabulary and Sentence Construction
The child:

- makes general statements and gives simple instructions, e.g.
  *It's a circle. No, it's too big.
  Put it there. Don't do that!
  Stop! You're wrecking it.*
- speaks in short, simple sentences

DEVELOPING

The child is beginning to develop cooperative behaviours and language during partner activities.

Text Content and Organisation
The child:

- makes simple plans with partner, e.g.
  We'll build a bridge. Where will we start?
- relies on teacher support to negotiate and solve problems, e.g.
  Child: *We want to build a tower but he won't share the big blocks.*
  Teacher: *Have a talk first.*

Vocabulary and Sentence Construction
The child:

- plans and negotiates using general terms, e.g.
  We'll have to start here. I'll go first, OK?
- use simple descriptions when interacting with partner, e.g.
  I've got a big circle. That's a little square.
- interacts spontaneously with partner in conversational style

CONSOLIDATING

The child demonstrates appropriate interactive behaviours and language when undertaking partner activities.

Text Content and Organisation
The child:

- incorporates joint planning and decision-making, e.g.
  *We could get ...
  Why don't we ...
  Do you know what we have to do?*
- uses language to negotiate and clarify roles, e.g.
  *Which part do you want to make?
  Who should do this?*

Vocabulary and Sentence Construction
The child:

- uses a range of vocabulary to plan, negotiate, monitor and reflect on the task, e.g. suggests ideas, gives instructions, challenges partner, evaluates task
- uses simple and complex sentences that incorporate vocabulary associated with the task
- interacts spontaneously and purposefully, e.g. through evaluative comments

EXPANDING

The child interacts confidently and successfully to complete partner activities.

Text Content and Organisation
The child:

- plans and sustains the interactive task, using language to negotiate and monitor each component
- reflects on the task to describe or evaluate the outcome

Vocabulary and Sentence Construction
The child:

- uses more specialised and technical vocabulary to plan and negotiate the task
- incorporates a variety of language forms to monitor the tasks, e.g.
  *This doesn't seem to be working.
  Have you got any more ideas?*
- reflects on the task using sophisticated vocabulary, e.g.
  *It was interesting when ....
  That was an excellent idea when ...*

PARTNER WORK

Indicators

BEGINNING

Responsiveness of Child as Speaker
The child:

- undertakes the interactive task in parallel with partner
- is usually silent
- has a dominant or passive pattern of interaction
- issues instructions or proceeds without consulting partner
- ignores partners' comments or reacts negatively
- begins task without planning

Responsiveness of Child as Listener
The child:

- makes few responses to speaker
- is unaware of need to respond to speaker during an interaction
- may answer questions but show little understanding of the task, e.g.
  Speaker: *Which part do you want to do?*
  Listener: *I like the yellow ones.*

DEVELOPING

Responsiveness of Child as Speaker
The child:

- uses a variety of verbal and non-verbal language to maintain cooperative behaviours
- begins to interact with partner, e.g. *I'll get some more big ones then we'll push it together.*
- may begin to take a more dominant role in the activity, e.g. *We have to put all the circles in this pile. I'll go first.*
- invites partner to join in the task, e.g. *I've done this bit. Do you want to do some now?*
- displays a more active interest in partner's involvement, e.g. *Hey, that's good. Let me do some.*
- begins to monitor the task
- makes simple, reflective comments

Responsiveness of Child as Listener
The child:

- begins to acknowledge the speaker by joining in planning, answering questions, making comments
- begins to interact to clarify the task
- answers to questions demonstrate an understanding of the task

CONSOLIDATING

Responsiveness of Child as Speaker
The child:

- discusses ideas before beginning activity, e.g.
  We could get some …
  Why don't we …
- talks and interacts during the task
- takes an equal role in the task, e.g. *We'll have to do this together or it will fall down.*
- includes partner in the activity, e.g. *Try this. I'll help you.*
- recognises partner's efforts, e.g. *That's a good idea. Now it should work.*
- makes initial plans and discusses ideas
- monitors the activity
- reflects on task and adds evaluative comments

Responsiveness of Child as Listener
The child:

- acknowledges the speaker through appropriate verbal and non-verbal responses
- interacts throughout the task by commenting, questioning and responding to questions
- monitors the speaker's comments or questions and adds appropriate information

EXPANDING

Responsiveness of Child as Speaker
The child:

- undertakes the task cooperatively
- recognises the value of talking to complete the task collaboratively, e.g.
  Let's stop and talk about what's happened.
- participates equally with partner
- negotiates tasks throughout activity
- seeks consensus
- reinforces partner's efforts
- monitors the task and adjusts accordingly
- reflects on outcome of completed task

Responsiveness of Child as Listener
The child:

- responds appropriately and confidently to partner's comments or questions
- monitors the interaction and adds comments or questions to sustain the activity-related talk
- uses highly developed interactive behaviour to ensure a successful completion of the partner activity

Section 2:

Inquiry

The Language of Inquiry

Questions serve many different purposes, take different forms and elicit responses of varying complexity.

In the classroom, teachers ask questions to carry on conversations, stimulate thinking, evaluate learning, initiate instruction, clarify ideas and ascertain what children know.

The questions children ask also play an important role in classroom learning. Children ask questions to obtain information, solve problems, clarify information with peers, check instructions and satisfy curiosity.

The types of questions asked provide teachers with insights into children's thinking. They reveal levels of understanding, indicate gaps in knowledge, and indicate stages of language development.

Contexts for Inquiry

- Questioning is a way of 'joining in'. It is a communicative tool used by speakers to initiate and maintain interaction with other people.

  Examples:
  - carrying on a conversation
  - including others in a discussion

- Questioning is a strategy used by active learners to gain information. It may be motivated by the need to have information for a particular purpose, or by curiosity and the 'need to know' for its own sake.

  Examples:
  - interviewing a community member
  - requesting instructions

- Questioning is a strategy used by active learners to clarify or confirm information.

  Examples:
  - questioning peers during a problem-solving activity
  - speculating on the outcome of an experiment

- Questioning is a strategy used by active learners to analyse and explore ideas. Questions we ask ourselves and other people are an important part of our thinking and reflection.

  Examples:
  - reflecting on a mathematics problem
  - analysing a story character's behaviour

In the upper primary school children's expertise in conducting interviews can also be used to enable them to collect oral histories.

Three strategies that will need to be further developed are:

- **Paraphrasing**: children learn to reflect back to people what they have said to ensure that the meaning has been effectively captured.

- **Questioning**: open-ended questioning techniques can be modelled and practised, such as 'Can you tell me more about ..?'

Teaching Strategies

Questioning

Question Role Play

Role playing involves children or adults putting themselves in someone else's position and speaking and behaving in a manner considered appropriate to that person or character. Usually speech and actions are unscripted and unrehearsed.

Teachers can use a variety of role play situations as an effective strategy for developing questioning skills with younger children. The technique requires children to discuss a storybook character as played by the teacher.

Example:

Read and discuss the story *Goldilocks and the Three Bears*. Display related props such as charts, story maps or masks. When the children are familiar with the story, introduce a baby bear finger puppet and role play the character. Involve the children in talking to, or questioning, the puppet, e.g. *We're going to ask Baby Bear about his garden. You might be able to tell him some interesting things about your garden as well.*

Brian:	*Have you got daisies?*
Teacher:	*Yes, he says he's got some daisies planted along the back fence. Uh huh, uh huh (while baby bear is whispering answer in teacher's ear). He and mother bear planted them. He likes to make daisy chains out of them. And do you know what he does? Instead of hanging the daisy chains around his neck, he hangs them off his ear (laughter from the children).*
Ryan:	*Has he got a sandpit?*
Teacher:	*Yes, mother bear and father bear dug a sandpit for him under the trees. Baby bear plays there nearly every day.*
David:	*Have you got any buckets and spades?*
Teacher:	*Well yes, he did have, but one day he got really mad and hit one of the trees with his spade and broke it.*
David:	*I want to ask what colour his bucket is. I've got a green bucket.*

This activity can be repeated using the same characters with different topics, e.g. favourite food, toys, clothes. Less intensive sessions, with different characters and themes, can be introduced later in the year (refer *Language and Literacy* chapter).

Teaching Points

- Place equal emphasis on seeking and sharing information. Elaborate answers and invite children to share information from their own experiences.
- Avoid highly structured turn-taking. Rather, encourage informal discussion and interaction.
- Extend minimum question-answer exchanges by providing children with the opportunity to interact with the puppet when asking questions.

Linking to Writing

At the conclusion of a role-play session, have children illustrate information gained through questioning. The child, or teacher, can add a sentence to the completed picture.

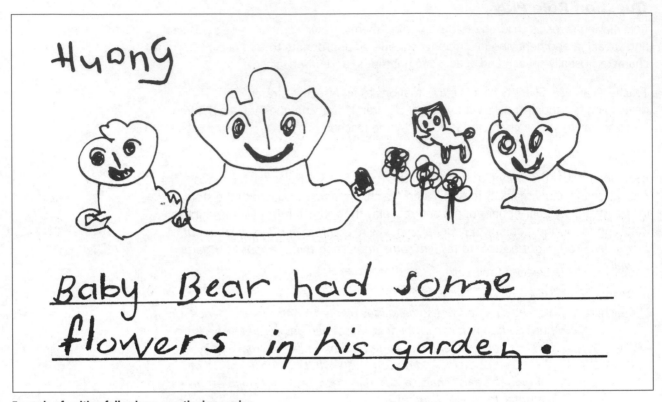

Huong

Baby Bear had some flowers in his garden.

Example of writing following a questioning session

Question Circle

Children's effectiveness in asking and answering questions will increase if they are involved in situations that require the use of questions and responses. The question circle strategy is designed to assist children to understand the role of questioning and answering in eliciting or providing information. Activities involve teacher modelling and support for those children who need explicit instruction in generating and asking effective questions. The strategy also encourages students to extend and refine their responses to a range of topic-related questions.

Procedure

The three stages in the strategy are not prescriptive and can be adapted to suit the age or ability level of the children. They are suitable for both small or large groups.

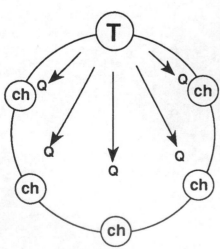

Resources: Topic cards related to familiar experiences such as birthdays, sport, toys or family. Use illustrations from magazines or select a topic card from Appendix 1 (pages 205–6).

Teacher-modelled Questions

Purpose: *To demonstrate how questions and answers are used to elicit or provide information.*

Steps:
- Introduce the purpose of the session; i.e. to ask some questions to gain information about the children.
- Display a topic card, discuss the pictures, then ask related questions around the circle.

- Compare and discuss children's answers.
- As children become more familiar with the routine, invite them to the 'question spot' to ask questions around the group.

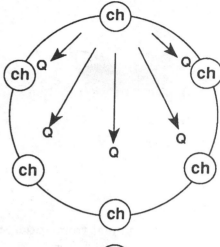

Teacher-facilitated Questions

Purpose: *To involve the children in generating a range of questions with teacher support.*

Steps:
- Instruct the children to choose a topic card and brainstorm topic-related questions, e.g. *when, who, where, what, why, would …*
- Support the activity with modelled questions and, if necessary, give specific prompts, e.g. *Who can think of a good 'why' question? What is a question we could ask to find out about…?*
- Children take turns in the 'question spot' and ask their prepared question around the circle. Don't attempt to cover all topics in one session. Treating fewer topics in depth will encourage more thoughtful and sophisticated questions.

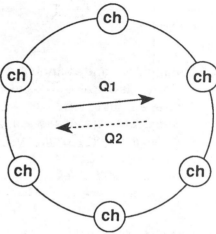

Independent Questions

Purpose: *To involve the children in generating questions without teacher support.*

Steps:
- Select a topic card.
- Place emphasis on generating follow-up questions from information supplied in answers. This approach encourages creative, original questions by challenging children to react to the speaker's feedback.

Teaching Points

- Highlight the terms 'question' and 'answer'. Explain that the purpose of questions is to elicit information. Give children examples of when we need to ask and answer questions.
- Discuss the need to use the person's name before addressing a question.
- Discuss the need to look at each other when asking and answering questions.
- Encourage children, through their questions, to explore different aspects of the topic. Monitor the quality of questions and intervene if they are becoming empty or imitative.
- Encourage children to elaborate answers. Summarise some of the interesting things mentioned in children's answers and discuss them with the group.
- Encourage as much discussion and interaction as possible so that questioning and answering happens in a natural, conversational context.

Group Interviews

An interview is usually conducted in a one-to-one situation where the interviewer asks questions to elicit information. In classrooms, the technique can be adapted to involve the whole class in interviewing one person. This approach allows children to work collaboratively to plan questions, practise the interview format and evaluate the effectiveness of their performance.

Children should always have an opportunity to practise the interview session with people they know, before guests are invited to the school.

Children's interviewing skills will develop as they are provided with situations in which questioning and critical listening are related to a specific purpose. The most effective way of promoting a meaningful context is through interviews linked across the curriculum.

Examples from Social Studies	Teaching Points

CHANGE
 	
Year 3
 	
Communities and Change
• Change takes place in communities as new ideas are put to use.
Subject Matter: *Changes in the local community and in contrasting communities, since early settlement, e.g. in buildings, transport or lifestyles.*
 	
DECISION MAKING
 	
Year 5
 	
Community Decisions
• Communities choose decision-makers.
• Community decision-makers help to provide services and facilities.
Subject Matter: *Local government.*
 	
Year 6
 	
Government
• People elect others to represent them in Parliament.
• Governments make decisions about providing services and facilities.
Subject Matter: *The State Parliament, State elections and functions of Government.*
	Interviews
	• develop the understanding that interviews need to be carefully planned to gain maximum benefit
	• develop the understanding that interview questions may address a range of issues relevant to a topic
	• teach children that in interviews, the interviewer often generates additional questions that encourage the person being interviewed to elaborate on earlier responses
	• teach children that questionnaires are a written form of interviews
	• teach children to formulate questions which require more than yes/no responses.
	
	Expositions and Debates
	• teach children that in an oral exposition they present one point of view which consists of:
	  - a statement of the point of view
	  - supporting arguments
	  - reiteration of main points
	• help children to understand that there can be more than one point of view on different issues
	• teach children to present oral and written expositions in which they:
	  - develop an argument
	  - present logical supporting arguments
	  - reiterate main points
	
	Reports
	• provide opportunities for children to plan, present and critique oral and written reports.
	
	Summaries
	• provide opportunities for children to present oral and written summaries
	• help children identify key words
	
	Notes
	• provide opportunities for children to make notes

Procedure
- Input

  This is the stage in which children gather information and engage in experiences that provide content for planning the interview. For example, Year 3 children may be studying *Communities and Change*. Information can be gathered through excursions, films, videos, reference books, charts, stories and discussion. Meaningful activities help children to relate previous knowledge to current information and provide a basis for planning interview questions to provide additional insights into the topic.

- Planning Questions

  Interviews provide a natural context for questioning. In an interview situation children practise effective questioning and develop communication skills related to critical listening. They learn that successful interviewers:
  - clarify the information they want to elicit and plan questions to achieve that outcome
  - ask relevant questions
  - listen to, and assess information, before formulating follow-up questions
  - rephrase questions to clarify misinterpretations
  - build onto previous questions to clarify or gain additional information.

- Brainstorming Questions

  Initially, teachers should work with the whole class to brainstorm questions related to the interview. A question framework can be used to organise information under *where, who, what, why, when, how* etc. Display the headings on a chalkboard or butcher's paper and record all questions suggested by the group (see illustration below). Discuss the questions and delete or refine examples that are too broad or only elicit a yes/no answer.

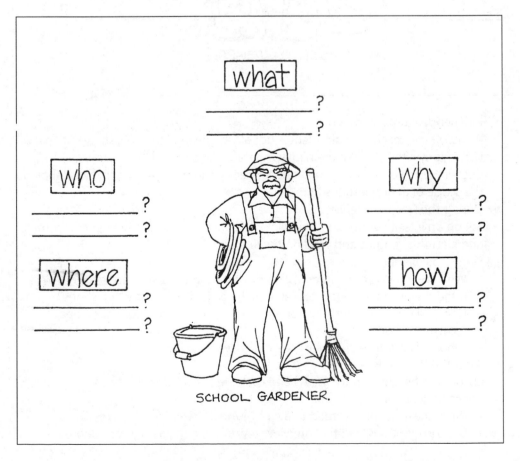

SCHOOL GARDENER.

- Topic-related Questions
More specific questions can be brainstormed by choosing particular topics related to the subject (see illustration below). The class, or small groups, may also provide sets of questions through discussion or research. Again, questions should be refined, deleted or elaborated until the class is satisfied they will elicit the most useful information.

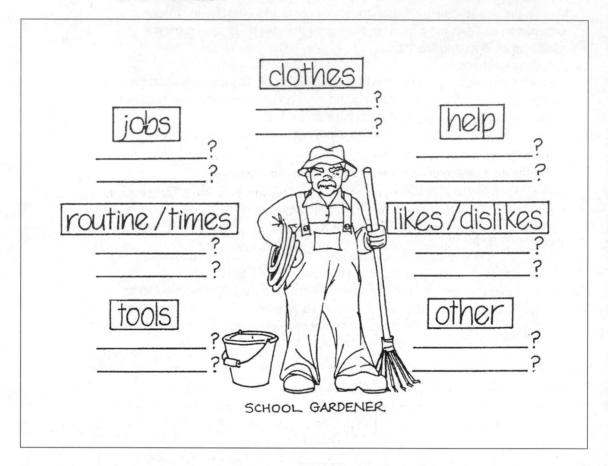

SCHOOL GARDENER

- Independent Brainstorming
At this stage, teacher involvement is not always needed to generate questions, particularly if the children are highly motivated or curious about a topic.
Encourage the children to work independently and provide support by extending the scope of their questions.
- During the Practice Interview
Set up an interview situation that allows children to practise the interview routine and identify strengths and weaknesses in their technique.
Points to consider:
  - Why are you doing the interview and what do you hope to achieve?
  - If there's more than one interviewer, who is going to ask the questions?
  - How will you record information? Consider notes, a questionnaire, tape recorder or video.
  - Who will introduce and thank the interviewee?
- After the Practice Interview
Encourage the children to discuss and evaluate the practice interview.
Points to consider:
  - Were the questions worded to avoid yes/no answers?
  - Did the questions lead the interview towards the required information?

– Were questions rephrased to clarify information?
– Were previous questions elaborated to gain more information?
– Did some of the answers provide ideas for follow-up questions?

At the conclusion of the reflection session, refine questions and make necessary modifications to the interview format. Send a copy to the invited guest to ensure the questions are acceptable. This strategy also provides time for the guest to focus on key questions, recall relevant information and prepare answers directly related to the questions. It also discourages the interviewee from providing all the information in response to the first question.

- Interviewing the Guest
  Encourage children to recall the main points discussed after the practice interview; for example:
  – Try to prompt full, interesting answers.
  – Don't rush! Give the person plenty of time to think about the question.
  – Try to make the person feel that you're interested in what is being said.
  – Try to 'steer' the interview towards the information you want.

Record the information through notes, a tape, video etc. (It is also a good idea to tell the interviewee how the information will be used.) At the conclusion of the interview, discuss the outcome and use the information gained in further planned activities, such as writing a report or preparing a radio talk.

Teaching Points
- Establish a clear purpose for asking questions and always link planning to a real interview.
- Monitor the content of children's questions. If they are becoming empty and stereotyped, suggest other areas to explore through questioning.
- Discuss the importance of active listening during the interview. Remind children to listen carefully to avoid repeating the same questions.
- Model how to use 'answer' information to generate follow-up questions.
- Model strategies for addressing problems that may arise during the interview, e.g. the interviewee who gives 'yes', 'no', or single-word responses, or the interviewee who uses technical vocabulary that can not be understood by the audience.
- Reinforce speaking and listening courtesies during the interview session.

Linking to Reading and Writing

Each stage of interviewing provides opportunities to develop a range of language skills. For example, children can take notes during research activities, edit questions, record interview responses and prepare a written report. The following table provides a format for planning.

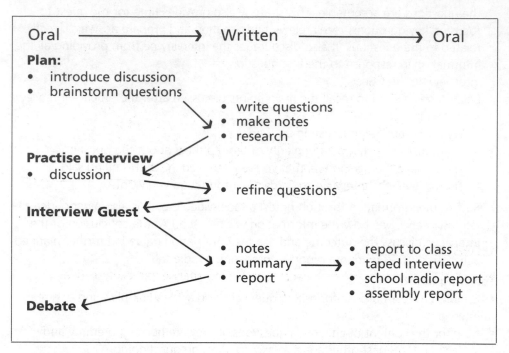

Individual Interviews

Provide opportunities for individual interviews when children have had experience in planning and conducting group interviews. Stress the importance of thorough preparation and encourage children to practise and review selected questions with a partner before beginning the final interview. The following ideas provide a process for planning.

- Find out some general information about the person's background.
- Decide on the purpose of the interview and explain this purpose to the person being interviewed.
- Think about how you will conduct the interview, e.g. some general questions to begin and a set list of questions that you want answered. Include questions that will give the person an opportunity to provide both short and long answers.
- Be prepared to add or delete questions as the interview progresses. Some information can be used to generate follow-up questions. Other information may answer more than one question on the list.
- Consider how the interview will be recorded; for example:
  – take notes or have a partner take responsibility for recording information
  – fill in a questionnaire
  – video the interview
- Don't rush. Give the person time to think and add extra information if desired.
- Try to word questions to avoid just a 'yes' or 'no' answer.
- Listen carefully to the answers as they will provide ideas for follow-up questions.
- Try to bring the interview to an end with an interesting question.

- Thank the person being interviewed and explain how the information will be used, e.g. for a report, newspaper article, local history project.

Creative Inquiry

Questioning is a strategy used by active learners to analyse and explore ideas. Teachers can encourage this type of questioning by modelling curiosity and reinforcing children's questions.

Display Table

Curiosity provides a natural motivation for questioning. Teachers can stimulate children's curiosity by providing a table or area for displaying new or unusual items. The following transcript describes kindergarten children interacting around an ocean display:

Tibor:	*Have a look (offering magnifying glass). It's a sea dragon.*
Yasmin:	*I know. What's this? (pointing to sea dragon's long beak)*
Tibor:	*I think it's a nose.*
Dimitri:	*(Picking up the sea dragon and inserting its beak into some coral with large holes.) What are the holes for? Maybe for its nose. It's stickybeaking coral.*

Children's spontaneous questions can be used to stimulate other children's thinking and promote further discussion and speculation. In the example below, the teacher took advantage of a child's interest in one of the items, and organised a science experiment. For example:

Stimulating Curiosity

↓

Sponge with interesting shape placed on table

↓

Child-initiated Question

I wonder what would happen if the sponge got wet?

↓

Investigations
- wetting the sponge
- cutting the sponge...
- pressing the sponge

Teaching Points
- Allow children to explore items independently before introducing and discussing them.
- Include resources that develop greater knowledge of the items, e.g. topic-related books or charts.
- Encourage ongoing investigation by supplying magnifying glasses, scales etc.
- Model curiosity and interest by picking up an item and commenting on it, e.g. *I wonder…*
- Follow a display of 'Common Objects' related to a theme with a display of 'Uncommon Objects'.
- Encourage children to share and discuss personal experiences related to the display table theme.

Linking to Writing
During a modelled writing session, discuss and write labels for items on the display table.

SPONGE

STARFISH

'Think About' Questions

The 'Think About' Questions strategy is based on a reading comprehension technique for answering literal and inferential questions. In the oral version children discuss a picture and brainstorm 'think about' questions that will assist in generating hypotheses about what is happening.

Procedure
The strategy has three stages. The second and third stages may need to be extended over more than one session.

- Partner Discussion
  The children sit with a partner and share what they notice about a picture. This initial activity stimulates lively discussion and encourages close observation of details. The discussion also helps later generation of questions and hypotheses about the picture. Partner sharing is followed by group sharing and discussion.
- Teacher-modelled Questions – 'Right There' and 'Think About
  At this stage the teacher models how to ask both types of questions.
  'Right There' and 'Think About' questions generate different levels of response. 'Right There' questions call for the children to identify obvious features in the picture, e.g. *What is the lady wearing?* 'Think About' questions require children to generate ideas and offer possible answers that go beyond the immediate information, e.g. *Why has the lady come into town?*

160

- Child-generated Questions and Hypotheses
  Children ask 'Think About' questions that are shared and discussed by the group. If children are having difficulty formulating questions, teachers can structure a more formal activity by writing some key question words on card; for example, *What, Where, When, Who, Why, How, Which*. The children then generate a question that begins with the key word on their card.

Variation-story version

At this stage, children should be offering many interpretations of what is happening in a picture. Select different versions to generate oral or written stories. Alternatively, carry out interviews where children answer 'think about' questions while role playing a picture character. This activity can be organised in pairs or small groups.

Question

Why is the man hiding behind the building? (Example of a 'Think About' question.)

Group Discussion

- *Maybe he's cold and he's standing out of the wind.*
- *He's waiting until the street is clear and then he's going to rush out and steal something.*
- *I think he's a policeman and he's watching this man over here.*
- *Maybe he's escaped from prison and he has to be careful nobody sees him.*
- *He's just had a haircut in the hairdresser's next door and he feels really silly and he doesn't want anyone to see him.*
- *I don't think he's hiding. He's just waiting for someone.*

Teaching Points

- Emphasise creative rather than correct questions and answers, e.g. *That's an interesting idea.*
- Be non-judgmental about children's answers. Accept all possibilities but ask children to substantiate their hypotheses whenever possible.
- Provide support for children who are not confident about offering ideas and opinions.
- Challenge children's thinking by offering contrasting ideas and perspectives.
- Talk about the influence of the media on people's thinking.
- Seize any opportunity to model a different perspective and use this to discuss alternative socio-cultural interpretations of situations and events.
- Illustrate that there are often 'multiple-readings' of situations and events.

Linking to Writing

Have children write their favourite story versions from the 'Think About' strategy.

Brainstorming Questions

This technique links effectively to social studies, science or health topics. Children begin by brainstorming topic-related questions using a 'Question Word' framework. Individually, with partners, or in a group, they research their question then report to the class. Forms of inquiry include library-based research, interviews, or practical investigations.

'School Rules' - Year 2

> **I Wonder**
>
> **Who**
>
> … who makes up the rules for the school?
> … who makes sure children are following the rules?
>
> **How**
>
> … how the school rules are made?
> … how rules have changed since Mum and Dad went to school?
> … how new children learn the rules?
>
> **When**
>
> … when people might forget the rules?
>
> **If**
>
> … if everyone in the school knows the rules?
> … if all schools have the same rules?
> … if the older children have any different rules?
>
> **Where**
>
> … where the school rules are written?
>
> **What**
>
> … what are the inside rules and outside rules?
> … what would happen if there weren't any rules?
> … what happens when people break rules?
>
> **Why**
>
> … why we have school rules?
> … why people break rules?

Example of topic-related questions

Teaching Points

- Don't impose constraints on children's spontaneous brainstorming. When brainstorming is finished, ask children to check their questions and eliminate any that are unclear or inappropriate.
- Discuss alternative strategies for researching questions and recording information.
- Encourage children to compare what they know before and after question brainstorming and discussion.
- Discuss other situations where you can use the strategy, e.g. planning a school camp.

Linking to Writing

1 Record questions during question brainstorming and share with the class.
2 Research questions by making notes or preparing a report.

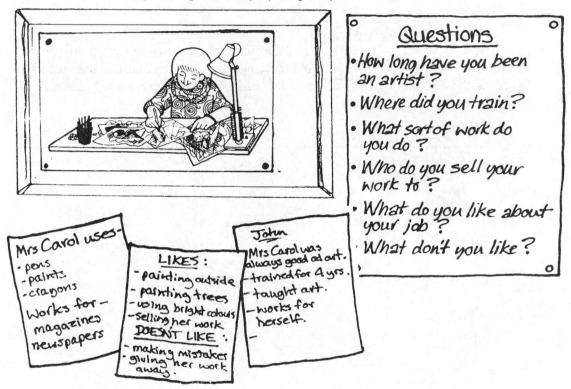

Questioning and Logic

The following strategy is based on the 'Twenty Questions' game that encourages logic-based questioning. In trying to identify an item, the children ask questions that can only be answered with 'Yes' or 'No'. This restriction encourages critical listening and thinking since the children must remember information supplied and choose further questions that eliminate as many alternatives as possible.

Procedure

Use a picture grid showing variations of an item (see Appendix 2 on pages 207–8). Pictures can be linked to curriculum topics or class themes.
Develop the strategy in three stages:

- Teaching the Game
  A child chooses an item in the array and the teacher models 'Yes'/ 'No' questions that will help identify it. If the answer is 'No' the child covers the eliminated items with a marker or block.

- Independent Questioning
  Children generate questions informally or take turns around a circle. This works well with small or whole-class groups. At the end of the game, children discuss the effectiveness of the questions and whether alternative questions could have been asked.

- Information Hunt
  This stage calls for independent questioning by each child. Provide each with a copy of the grid. Pin another, with one item marked, on each child's back. To identify the marked item, the children move around the class asking 'Yes', 'No' questions. Eliminated items are crossed out on the recording sheet. With large groups, change the format by seating the class around five or six children. Children with picture grids complete the game by questioning around the circle.

Explore the use of:

- Questions for Reflection
  'what worked best?'
  'how did we ...?'
  'what might we have done?'

- Questions for clarification
  'I wonder why you chose the triangular shape?'
  'Why do you feel so strongly about mining rights?'

Teaching Points

- Children's attempts to generate questions often reveal gaps in vocabulary and background knowledge. Improve questioning techniques by modelling.
- Discuss why some questions are more effective than others. Draw children's attention to 'empty' questions; in other words, questions that don't elicit much information—use examples from your own questions, not those offered by children.
- Make listeners aware of the need to indicate when they don't understand the question. Help children to modify unclear questions.
- Some children have difficulty using 'Yes'/ 'No' answers to eliminate items. After questioning, check that the correct item has been eliminated. If necessary, repeat or rephrase the information.

Linking to Writing

Construct 'What Am I?' and 'Who Am I?' quizzes by formulating and writing
information based on the questioning game.

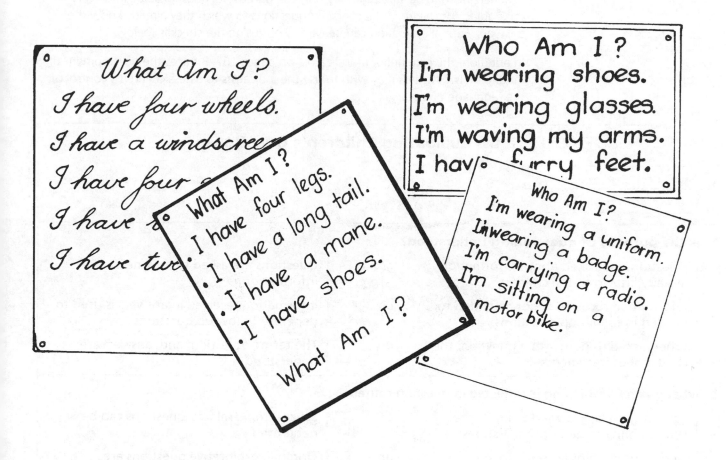

What Am I?
I have four wheels.
I have a windscreen
I have four
I have
I have two

What Am I?
• I have four legs.
• I have a long tail.
• I have a mane.
• I have shoes.

What Am I?

Who Am I?
I'm wearing shoes.
I'm wearing glasses.
I'm waving my arms.
I have furry feet.

Who Am I?
I'm wearing a uniform.
I'm wearing a badge.
I'm carrying a radio.
I'm sitting on a motor bike.

Assessment

The importance of modelling the use of questioning cannot be over estimated. Teachers need to be sure that they only ask purposeful questions. It can be very misleading for children if teachers ask questions to which they already know the answers. Formal evaluation can be carried out using the checklist below.

In addition, the continuum of indicators on pages 167–8 traces the development of inquiry skills. Teachers may wish to use the indicators to assess children's control of the language of inquiry.

Criteria for Evaluating Children's Questions

Name: _____

Date: _____

Class: _____

1 Is the purpose of questioning understood?

☐ Questions are asked about information already known to the child	*or*	☐ Questions are asked to seek new information
☐ Information received is not attended to, or used in follow-up questions	*or*	☐ Information received in answers is used to generate follow-up questions
☐ When asked to generate a question, the child makes statements	*or*	☐ The terms, 'question' and 'answer' are understood

2 What quality of thinking is reflected in question content?

☐ Lack of general knowledge limits the child's ability to generate questions	*or*	☐ Several topic-related questions can be generated
☐ Questions are highly concrete and predictable	*or*	☐ Original, explorative questions are generated

3 What language structures does the child use?

☐ Help is needed to formulate the question	*or*	☐ Questions are grammatically well-formed
☐ There is a reliance on familiar, overlearned patterns	*or*	☐ A variety of question forms is used

4 Are the conventions of communication being observed?

☐ It is unclear to whom the child is addressing the question	*or*	☐ Appropriate strategies are used to attract the attention of the person with whom the child wishes to communicate
☐ There is little verbal or non-verbal interaction beyond the exchange of question and answer	*or*	☐ The child provides feedback: • if the question is not understood; • if the answer does not include the requested information; and • to acknowledge that an answer has been received

I N Q U I R Y

Inquiry relates to the asking and answering of questions to serve a range of purposes.

Indicators

BEGINNING

The child has a limited understanding of the role of questioning in eliciting responses or information.

Text Content and Organisation
The child:

- is unaware of the role of question words—when, who, where, what, why—in gaining information
- relies on teacher support to formulate questions to elicit information, e.g. *I'm finished?* rather than, *Have I finished?*

Vocabulary and Sentence Structure
The child:

- uses statements rather than question formats to elicit information, e.g. *It's big?*
- uses questions that are highly-practised or predictable, e.g. *What colour is it? Do you like it?*
- formulates questions about known information, e.g. *Is it big?*
- uses a range of learned question formats for more formal classroom situations, e.g. during newstelling, only asks *Where did you get it?* and *Do you like it?*

DEVELOPING

The child incorporates a limited range of question formats to elicit responses or information.

Text Content and Organisation
The child:

- uses question words—when, who, where, what, why, how—to gain and clarify information
- formulates simple questions in informal and formal situations, e.g. during activity time and newstelling sessions
- relies on teacher support to formulate questions that will provide extended information, e.g. during class reports

Vocabulary and Sentence Structure
The child:

- begins to use a range of vocabulary relating to question formats, e.g. when, who, where, what, why, did, can
- responds to the situation by formulating simple but appropriate question formats to elicit information, e.g. *What happened next? So what did you do?*
- practises a range of question formats in more formal activities, e.g. *How did you make it? What did you use?*

CONSOLIDATING

The child uses a range of question forms for different purposes and to stimulate responses of varying complexity.

Text Content and Organisation
The child:

- generates several topic-related questions to sustain the conversation or discussion
- interprets and responds to information received by formulating further questions during a partner discussion of a maths activity
- includes literal, inferential or evaluative questions during planned classroom activities, e.g. when interviewing a story-book character

Vocabulary and Sentence Structure
The child:

- incorporates question formats that elicit literal, inferential or evaluative information, e.g. *How many ... What would have happened if ... How did you feel about ...*
- interprets and responds to information received by formulating appropriate follow-up questions, e.g. *So, what did you do next?*
- adapts question formats to suit informal and formal situations, e.g. spontaneous interaction during a conversation as opposed to monitoring a class report before shaping questions

EXPANDING

The child uses questioning to stimulate and extend thinking, gain information and elicit responses of varying complexity.

Text Content and Organisation
The child:

- shapes questions to produce optimal information, e.g. during an interview
- reflects on information and generates speculative questions as a strategy for solving problems, e.g. during science experiments—*What if we ... I wonder ... what will happen when ...*
- lists the types of questions that will elicit required information, e.g. *I'll need to ask, when, who, why about information*
- stimulates and extends own thinking by questioning to explore possibilities, and make links between previous and new knowledge

Vocabulary and Sentence Structure
The child:

- generates questions that are grammatically well-formed and appropriate to the situation
- generates 'closed' questions as an efficient strategy to obtain necessary information, e.g. *Where is the book? What colour do you want?*
- generates 'open' questions to elicit a range of responses, e.g. *Why should we ... How would you ...*
- uses a range of literal, inferential or evaluative question formats to suit informal or formal situations, e.g. group discussions, class interview debating

Indicators

I N Q U I R Y

BEGINNING

Responsiveness of Child to Speaker
The child:

- makes statements when asked to generate a question
- asks questions about established information
- needs teacher support to respond to information received, e.g. to generate a follow-up question
- asks questions that are 'learned' or highly predictable
- asks 'closed' questions that involve limited use of language and require little thought, e.g. *What colour is it?*

Responsiveness of Child Listener
The child:

- has sufficient knowledge of the topic to respond to the question
- responds with one or two word answers
- uses little verbal or non-verbal interaction beyond the exchange of questions and answers
- needs teacher support to respond to the question

DEVELOPING

Responsiveness of Child to Speaker
The child:

- begins to generate simple question formats, e.g. *when, who, where, what, why*
- asks simple questions that relate to information required
- needs some teacher support and prompting to respond to information received, e.g. to generate a follow-up question
- uses questions spontaneously during informal interactions
- uses a small range of practised question formats during more formal situations, e.g. class sharing sessions
- needs teacher support to use 'open' questions, e.g. when completing a character study

Responsiveness of Child Listener
The child:

- has sufficient knowledge of the topic to respond to the question
- provides a simple response to the question
- provides feedback if the question is not understood, e.g. *What do you mean?*
- responds to the question and may provide follow-up information if the questioner seeks clarification

CONSOLIDATING

Responsiveness of Child to Speaker
The child:

- uses question formats that elicit literal, inferential or evaluative comments in classroom related activities, e.g. identifying character traits, reporting on science experiments
- formulates questions that provide a range of information, e.g. an explanation, a comparison, a justification
- uses questions spontaneously in informal situations, e.g. to carry on a conversation, clarify ideas, gain information
- formulates both open and closed questions to gain information and extend thinking
- needs teacher support to plan and complete more formal activities, e.g. interviewing, simple debates

Responsiveness of Child Listener
The child:

- provides information beyond a simple response, if required, e.g. limited information for a closed question and extended information for an open question
- interacts with questioner until sufficient information is provided
- interacts spontaneously in informal situations
- begins to monitor more formal activities, e.g. anticipates types of questions that will be asked during an interview

EXPANDING

Responsiveness of Child to Speaker
The child:

- uses questions for a range of purposes, e.g. to communicate, to explore social and personal development, and to extend thinking
- uses a range of questioning techniques to produce optimal information, e.g. closed questions for key points and open questions to stimulate thought and a variety of responses
- uses questions as a strategy to locate information, e.g. *If I'm studying animals, I can ask questions about location, eating habits, classification* etc.
- interprets and responds to information received by generating questions to extend the topic
- independently plans and completes activities in more formal situations, e.g. community interview, formal debates

Responsiveness of Child Listener
The child:

- provides information that extends beyond a simple response, e.g. provide details and an opinion
- monitors and responds to the direction of the interaction, e.g. predicts the types of follow-up questions that will be asked and incorporates information in planned responses
- interacts spontaneously and confidently for a range of purposes and audiences, e.g. during conversations, discussions and meetings
- responds effectively and confidently during formal situations, e.g. interviews, debates

Section 3:

Classification

Language plays an integral part in developing knowledge. From an early age children learn to explore and interpret experiences. They label objects, people and events. They also talk about the features of objects and make mental comparisons between past and new experiences.

Children move through observable phases of development as they acquire classification skills.

- There is poor comprehension of the classification task. No consistent classification strategy is evident. The child may generalise inappropriately from personal experience, e.g. idiosyncratic observations:

  That hat and the towel go together because they are not too big.

  That hat goes with the basket because you put the hat in the basket.

- Little language is initiated during the task. Gaps in vocabulary knowledge are evident.

- The child sorts items on the basis of concrete features, e.g. function, attributes. There is an exploratory approach to the task that involves switching criteria during classification. Often the task does not reach completion stage; for example:

  They both move.
  Let's put the heat stuff together.
  It's got some plastic and some glass.

- Language is used more actively as a tool for thinking. The child labels, describes and explains.

PHASE 3
- The classification task is completed quickly and efficiently with clear understanding of goals. The child self-monitors and corrects inappropriately grouped items, for example:

  I'll put this on the table. This is going to be the glass section.
  Cassettes are glass – no, plastic.
  The radio doesn't belong. It has to go in a separate place.
  They're weapons – things that kill people.
  Have you got anything that matches?

- Talk is used to develop a critical, reasoned understanding of the task. More complex language is evident, e.g. definitions and generalisations are included. The child may also use specific terminology related to classification, e.g. match, group.

The Language of Classification

To compare objects or make groups, children need to engage in labelling and description. When children and adults talk about objects and experiences they use the following criteria.

Perceptual Criteria

size	parts
shape	materials
colour	features
texture	

Knowledge Criteria

location	habits
function	actions
operation	properties
characteristics	family group

Evaluative Criteria

usefulness	quality
value	condition
attractiveness	safety
interest level	suitability
durability	fashion

The facility for comparison is in-built into our language:

> *more … than*
> *better than … because*
> *the (…) est one*
> *the same as …*
> *not as …*
> *quite …, very …, a bit …*

Contexts for Classification

As children develop they have less need to deal with concrete objects in order to think about them. Networks of knowledge become more extensive and sophisticated, and language becomes an essential tool in organising this knowledge. Classroom contexts provide excellent environments in which children can make this transition from the concrete to the abstract. For example, children learn abstract labels, such as 'Animals' or 'The Seasons' to refer to classes of objects or events. They also use language to make generalisations about the world; for example, 'Summer and winter are the hottest and coldest seasons'.

The strategies in this section are used in contexts that encourage children to use talk in the observation and reasoning processes associated with classification. Some strategies involve highly-structured, 'hands on' activities that provide an effective starting point for kindergarten children. Others, such as semantic grids and knowledge maps, require more abstract thinking.

Initially, some children may need assistance to use oral language for effective learning during classification activities. For instance, they may need to be shown how to talk through observations in order to make objective, reasoned decisions. Providing this support increases children's general knowledge, develops logical thinking skills and teaches an active, powerful approach to learning.

- Classification is an important component of classroom learning.
- Classification experiences provide a context for organising and understanding the world.
- Classification activities promote the language of definition, generalisation and abstraction.

Children who engage in talking as part of their natural, exploratory learning style are well prepared for the challenging tasks associated with formal learning.

Teaching Strategies

Comparing and Grouping

Simple Sorting and Grouping Activities

An important prerequisite for classification is the ability to note similar and different features about items and develop vocabulary to describe these features.

The following activities involve groups of items that belong in the same category but have some contrasting features. The tasks develop both observational skills and descriptive language. Purposeful contexts across the curriculum can be devised for such activities.

Materials
Any group of items that have contrasting features:
food, buttons, dinosaurs, shells, leaves, shoes etc.

Containers or other aids for sorting:
lengths of wool, hoops, bowls, ice-cream containers etc.

Sorting
With a partner or in small groups, sort items into ice-cream containers. Encourage children to devise names for each group, e.g. *Spider shells, Trumpet shells.*

Devising groups or 'families'
As a class, define groups based on special features, such as:
Fan shells – ridges, smooth inside, shaped like a fan
Abalone – a rainbow inside, row of holes on edge

When children engage in classification activities as part of social studies or science themes, provide additional information in reference books, charts and picture collections.

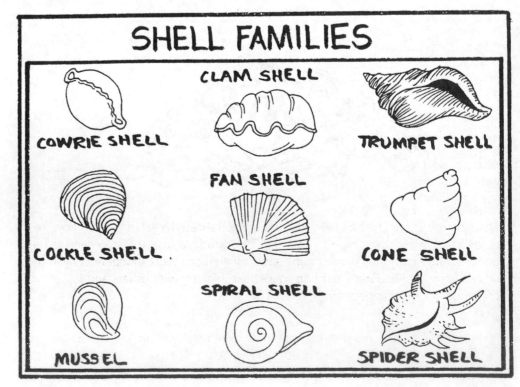

Guessing Games

Use familiar guessing game formats such as the 'feely bag' to practise descriptions; for example: *I think it's a trumpet shell because it's pointy at the top and has a hole at the bottom.*

Model how to make groups and ask the children to guess what they are. Teacher modelling is an effective way of extending children's thinking beyond obvious classification features, e.g. *Why do you think I put these together?*

Sorting into Two Groups

Provide a selection of items and ask the children to make two groups. Items which do not fit the selected criteria can be excluded. Children write, or the teacher scribes, group names.

Matching Games

Finding matching items is a simple classification task that can be used before more complex classification activities.

The criteria used to link items reveal children's developmental levels. Three strategies for making pairs are commonly used by young children:

- simple 'association by use' links, such as,
  You eat with your knife and fork;
- pairing items with an obvious visual feature, such as,
  They've both got an orange bit; and
- a created story link, such as,
  A car and a boat go together because you drive your car and then you could go on the boat.

Later, children begin to understand the concept of matching on the basis of features in common. They also become less reliant on obvious perceptual features and show evidence of more abstract reasoning, e.g. *Cars and boats are both transport things.*

Teachers can move children towards a more sophisticated level of performance by modelling the thinking process involved in classifying. At first, this may need to be demonstrated with the whole group. Later, children can work independently in pairs or small groups. Encourage them to share their thinking with others and to challenge and substantiate decisions.

Pairs

Place pictures or objects in an array and discuss which items can be paired. If children are working at a higher concrete level, select materials that can be linked by simple 'function' or 'association by use' criteria.

173

Modified 'Snap'

To play this game, the children need to work in pairs. First, place picture cards, face down, in the middle of the group. The first pair then turns over two cards and attempts to justify a link between the pictures. If there is group acceptance, the pair may keep the cards. If not, the cards are returned to the middle. During the game, encourage group challenges and discussion.

The activity is also suitable for groups of three children. In this version, two children play while the third child judges whether the justifications are reasonable.

Picture Association

The object of this activity is to develop flexible and creative thinking. It can be played using a collection of objects or pictures, or developed during a brainstorming and scribing session. To play, add one item at a time to a sequence, then justify each subsequent addition by describing a feature which can be shared with the previous item. For example, in an animal sequence, a cow might be placed beside a horse because both have four legs; a chicken might be placed next to the cow because both are farm animals; and an eagle might be placed next to the chicken because both have feathers.

Comparison Activities

Comparison activities are an excellent strategy for encouraging close observations of objects. These observations, in turn, promote description and comparison which are fundamental to classification.

Partner Activities

Children begin by drawing pictures about themselves and then discussing similarities and differences. This basic game concept can be adapted in a variety of ways. For example, children may draw their house, family car, school bag or bike, and then compare them. Children can also share and compare information about themselves during a partner discussion activity. Possible topics include hobbies, routines, holiday activities, toys or favourite books.

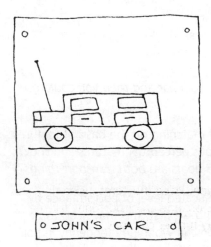

JOHN'S CAR

CAROL'S CAR

Missing Item

Tell a story about a child who loses a belonging or item of clothing during a school excursion. Describe the item in detail. In the next part of the story, explain how the child's parents buy a replacement. They cannot find the exact item, but manage to find one that is nearly the same. Ask the children to draw the new item, and then describe how it is similar or different from the original; for example:

Well, the new jumper was still in the Adelaide Crows colours, but it wasn't as thick, and it felt a bit scratchy.

Vary the theme for the activity, e.g. Lost Pet, Broken Toy.

The Lost Dinosaur

(Sloan and Latham, Macmillan, 1985)

The text is about a lost baby dinosaur. During his travels he meets many different dinosaurs before finding his mother.

When reading the story, ask the children to substantiate why each new dinosaur cannot be the parent; for example:

The baby dinosaur has a crest on its head but this dinosaur doesn't.

This dinosaur has scales on its back. This one has bumps but they're not scales.

More Complex Grouping Activities

The activities described in the section 'Simple Sorting and Grouping Activities' (pp. 172–3), require children to group objects that belong together. This is done on the basis of simple perceptual features such as colour, shape or texture.

Classification differs from sorting in the level of abstraction in criteria used to make groupings. For example, in order to decide whether an animal should be classified as plant-eating or meat-eating, the child cannot rely simply on grouping items that look the same (i.e. sorting); relevant background knowledge is also required.

The ability to handle more abstract classification tasks marks an important developmental movement. Discussion can play an important role in this shift since talking elicits background knowledge about the items being classified and encourages children to explore different ways of classifying.

Materials:

Collections of pictures or objects; for example:

* *kitchen utensils*
* *fabric and craft materials*
* *'shop' items, such as packets, tins*
* *picture sets, such as clothes, animals, transport*
* *cut-outs from shop catalogues*
* *objects collected during nature walks*

Making Groups

Distribute a set of pictures or objects for classification. Place the items inside rings, or record the groupings on paper. During the activity, provide an opportunity for the children to explain their groupings and to make any further changes.

Variations

* Model a classification activity without a verbal explanation of the grouping. In this version, the class must guess why objects have been grouped together.
* Before a classification activity nominate the number of groups that must be made.
* Organise the children to work independently and allow swapping of items between tables.

Making Pyramids

Making a 'pyramid' or 'classification tree' is an activity in which children divide sets of information into subsets. Initially, model the process during whole-group activities. The idea is to sort a set of items into two groups, such as living and non-living. Next, divide new groups into two parts, such as animal and plant, or artificial and natural. Continue the process until all the items have separate 'branches'.

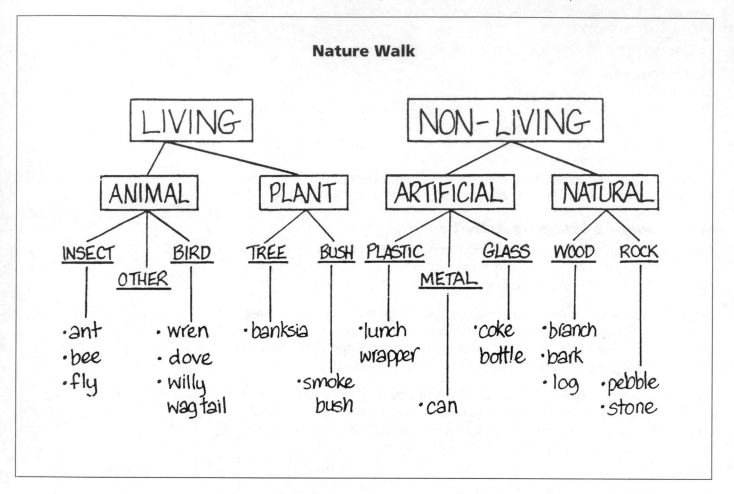

Classification Books

Make theme books based on classification activities. These can be produced as individual scrapbooks or a shared book.

Classification Mural

In this activity the children prepare a classification chart related to a curriculum topic or theme. First, collect relevant pictures and attach strips of adhesive paper for easy movement and grouping. Next, discuss and decide on the most appropriate groups. Attach each section to the classification chart and add suitable headings.

The activity is also valuable when extended into partner or 'free-choice' sessions. As well, it offers an opportunity to make informal observations of children's classification skills.

Brainstorming and Building Knowledge

Collections

Use individual or classroom collections to introduce sorting and classification.

Individual Presentations

Organise a roster, or ask for volunteers to bring items related to hobbies or interests. These might include badges, Tee-ball gear, favourite books, stamps or toys. Provide time for the children to label the items, set up a display and make a brief presentation to the class or a small group.

Display Table

Choose a theme and ask each child to contribute an item for the display table. Use the collection for discussion and classification activities.

Whole-school activities

Use 'dress-up' or 'theme-days' as a fun way of introducing a variety of classification activities. Examples are 'Red Day', 'Story Character Day' or 'International Day'.

Dress-up day

Knowledge Maps

Making a 'knowledge map' is a brainstorming technique using classification frameworks generated by the teacher or class. It can be introduced during an intensive brainstorming session or developed while a topic is being researched. The following examples range from simple, highly-concrete frameworks suited to pre-primary children, to more abstract frameworks designed for older students. Headings are introduced either at the beginning of the activity to guide brainstorming, or, after brainstorming, to organise information.

Guided Brainstorming

Include headings at the beginning of the activity to assist children in generating ideas.

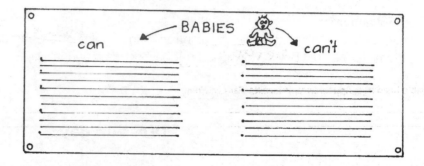

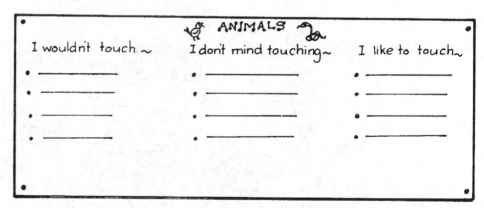

Free Brainstorming

Ask children to generate words or ideas about a chosen topic. Write them onto
separate cards or paper strips. Group the items and make headings.

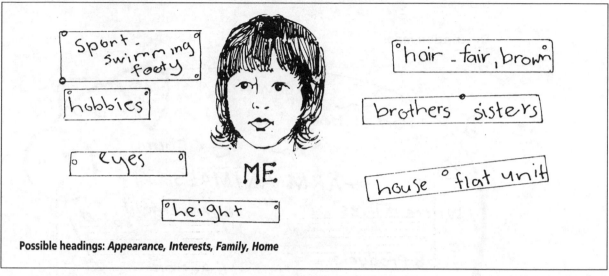

Sport - swimming footy

hobbies

eyes

ME

height

hair - fair, brown

brothers sisters

house flat unit

Possible headings: *Appearance, Interests, Family, Home*

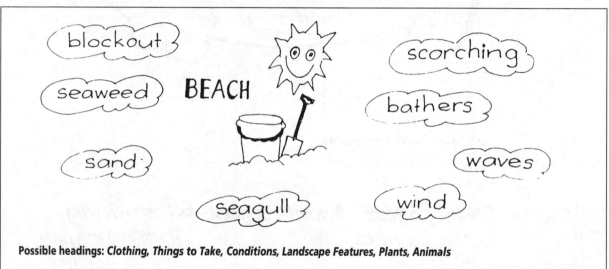

blockout

seaweed

sand

BEACH

seagull

scorching

bathers

waves

wind

Possible headings: *Clothing, Things to Take, Conditions, Landscape Features, Plants, Animals*

wings   basket   feathers

games   PETS   legs

water shell   seeds

tail   kennel

nest

Possible headings: *Appearance, Food, Homes*

Observation Frameworks

Important prerequisite skills for effective classification are observing and describing. Outlined below are three frameworks for structuring this knowledge-building process.

Description maps

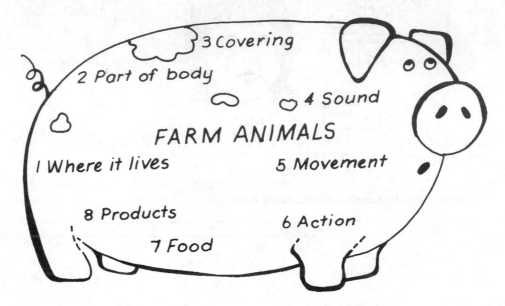

3 Covering

2 Part of body

4 Sound

FARM ANIMALS

1 Where it lives

5 Movement

8 Products

6 Action

7 Food

Modified news framework

COMPARE: 1. when   2. who   3. what it does   4. what for   5. where   6. how it works   7. why they are/ aren't useful

truck

car

Seeing, Knowing, Feeling...

Science report

My **object** is a

Answer the following questions:

    1 What is one thing you notice about the object?

    2 What is one thing you know about the object?

    3 What do you think about the object?

Now share with your partner. Can you add one more item of information to each question?

Now research your object in a book. Can you add two more items of information to Question 2?

Semantic Grids

The semantic grid is an effective strategy for developing text comprehension. Adapted as a classification strategy, it is also useful for consolidating mathematics, social studies or science topics. To complete the activity, children must think of items meeting the criteria that intersect on the grid (see grid examples below). The answers are drawn or written in the spaces provided.

	zoo	home
fur		
skin		

Simple Semantic Grid

The simplest semantic grids have a restricted number of criteria. Make the frameworks more complex by increasing the criteria and incorporating the need for more specialised knowledge.

	meat-eater	plant-eater
horns		
plates		
wings		
long neck		

Complex Semantic Grid

Semantic grids are successful as an individual, partner or group activity. They also provide an excellent, informal strategy for evaluating classification skills.

182

Variation

To extend thinking, leave out the headings on the grid. The children must then infer the missing headings from information supplied. This is a challenging activity, particularly suited to partner grouping.

Envoy

• The whole class can brainstorm a topic, e.g. the land

mountains	conservation	mining	cultivation	sandplain	habitat
real estate	water		trees	degradation	ecology
desert swamp	jungle	LAND	irrigation	islands	travel
arctic	land rights		continents		

• In four groups, words are classified into categories determined by each group:

• Each group adopts a category and sketches out a framework for study.

• Each group appoints an 'ENVOY' who is sent to another group to report on proceedings—ideas, suggestions, conclusions, decision.

• The envoy then listens to the report of the group she/he has reported to, and carries that information back to the home group.

Linking to Writing
The semantic grid activity also provides a planning framework for written descriptions and reports.

	Eats	Live	Colour	Special Features
Brown Bear	fish	Woods	Brown	he like to eat salmon
Polar Bear	Seals	norf poole	white	he has got fat on his back to cip him warm
Panda Bear	bab boo	chinu	black and white	he is a vejutered

Teaching Points
- Model activities with the whole group before introducing them as partner or small-group activities.
- Conduct brainstorming activities with the whole group to provide a greater number and variety of ideas.
- Accept all ideas in initial brainstorming sessions. Evaluative feedback at this stage can inhibit children's initiation of ideas. Later, revise brainstormed ideas, allowing children to decide what should be retained or deleted.
- Encourage children to use books and other resources to extend their knowledge of chosen topics.
- Extend children's vocabulary by modelling more specific terms; for example:
  Another word we use for an animal that is dangerous and lives in the jungle or bush is a 'wild' animal. What are some of the wild animals you can think of?
- Reinforce the meaning of abstract category terms; for example:
  So, in our requirements sections we talked about things that plants need to live. What are some of the requirements that human beings have?

Assessment

Monitor and record classification performance by organising independent activities based on classroom themes and curriculum topics. Many of the activities outlined in the section, such as semantic grids, are suitable for evaluation purposes.

When making any informal evaluations remember:

- performances are greatly influenced by the level of difficulty of materials provided
- the evaluation task only gives a sample of a child's performance relative to other class members
- one evaluation task is not an absolute measure of the child's classification skills.

The 'What to look for' list below suggests observational criteria for informally monitoring classification skills.

What to look for:

Do the children:

- **understand the classification task (i.e. abstracting features of similarity, such as dogs, cats and horses being animals)?**
- **ignore irrelevant perceptual features of objects when making groupings (e.g. all cars in the collection are red)?**
- **use appropriate naming and descriptive vocabulary during the classification task?**
- **go beyond obvious perceptual features such as colour, size and shape in making groupings?**
- **logically substantiate classification choices, e.g. *I put these together because they can all move?***
- **follow through classification criteria in a systematic way?**

The assessment task on pages 186–7 and scoring criteria on page 188 allow more formal evaluation.

In addition, the continuum of indicators on pages 189–190 traces the development of classification skills. Teachers may wish to use the indicators to assess children's control of the language of classification.

Classification Assessment Task

Materials:
12 picture cards of a variety of items, including at least three transport items, e.g. wagon, boat, towel, shirt, orange, church, gun, hat, spear, motorbike, basketball, car.

Procedure:

Part 1
Lay out the twelve picture cards in an array. Ask the child to name the pictures.

Part 2
Ask the child to make pairs and to explain his or her selections; for example:

> *I want you to find two things that could go together. They have to have something the same about them.*

Part 3
Display the transport pictures (wagon, motorbike, boat).

Question 1:

> *Why do you think I put these things together?*
> *What's the same about all of them?*

Question 2:

> *Yes, they are all things that you travel in, that move. What would be a good name for that group?*

Question 3:

> *Motorbikes, wagons and boats are all transport things – things that get you from one place to another. Can you think of some other transport things we could add to this group?*

Child: _____

Year Level: _____

Date: _____

Classification Data Sheet

Part 1
List any vocabulary which is not known.

Part 2
List pairs nominated and explanation given.

_____   _____   _____

_____   _____   _____

_____   _____   _____

_____   _____   _____

_____   _____   _____

_____   _____   _____

_____   _____   _____

Part 3
Record child's response to three questions.

Question 1: *(inferring criterion used to create group)*

Question 2: *(providing category name for group)*

Question 3: *(brainstorming items that belong to the category)*

Classification Scoring Sheet

Part 1

Score: 0   No vocabulary known

          1   Some unknown vocabulary

          2   All vocabulary known   (2)

_____

Part 2

Score: 0   Task not understood; irrelevant responses

          1   Association or 'story' links, e.g.:
                 The man got a hat then he got a basket.

          2   Nominates features of similarity, e.g.:
                 They've both got wheels.

          3   Uses abstract labels, e.g.:
                 They're weapons.

(Score four best responses .)   (12)

_____

Part 3

Question 1:

Score two points for appropriate, well-substantiated answer,   (2)
e.g., *'They move.'; 'You go places in them'.*   _____

Question 2:

Score two points for the term 'transport'.   (2)

_____

Question 3:

Score two points if the child generates three or more items   (2)
without assistance.   _____

       TOTAL   (20)

_____

Overall Rating: 0–4 low; 5–9 low-average; 10–14 average; 15–20 strong

Indicators

CLASSIFICATION

BEGINNING

The child makes arbitrary selections when grouping. No classification strategies are evident.

Text Content and Organisation
The child:

- initiates little information
- needs teacher support to label or describe items

Vocabulary and Sentence Construction
The child:

- uses general labels, e.g. dog, apple
- makes unrelated links between items, e.g.
  The hat goes with the basket because you put the hat in the basket.
- makes simple statements, e.g.
  That's a hat.
  It's a dress.

Responsiveness of Child as Speaker
The child:

- relies on teacher prompting and questioning to classify items, e.g.
  Can you find the things that belong together? Can you put each group in its special box?
- completes classification tasks with minimal talking or interaction
- relies on teacher prompts to describe or explain how items have been sorted or focuses on labelling the items rather than describing the relationship between the items, e.g.
  That's a horse. That's a cow, rather than, They're all animals.

DEVELOPING

The child forms groups using a 'trial and error' approach. Items are sorted using simple criteria, e.g. function, attributes.

Text Content and Organisation
The child:

- includes labels and some descriptions, e.g.
  They're trucks. They have big wheels and they're heavy.
- links ideas with an attribute that may not have a logical link to the classification, e.g.
  The ice-cream goes with the teddy because they are both small

Vocabulary and Sentence Construction
The child:

- uses more detailed labelling, e.g. parts of vehicles or plants
- uses simple, descriptive language, e.g. shape, colour, size
- uses vocabulary and sentence construction that link attributes and function, e.g.
  They've got wheels and a motor and you drive in them.

Responsiveness of Child as Speaker
The child:

- needs teacher support and questioning to describe features of items and reasons for classifications
- begins to incorporate talking and interaction to complete classification activities
- begins to incorporate descriptions of items when classifying groups
- describes simple relationship between items, e.g.
  They all swim in the water. (prompt) They are sea creatures

CONSOLIDATING

The child's sorting skills are more consistent and show evidence of self-monitoring. Subgroups are described and items are sorted using consistent criteria.

Text Content and Organisation
The child:

- labels and describes items fully
- shows logical links between items and classification decisions, e.g.
  The caravan should go with this group because it's a type of shelter.

Vocabulary and Sentence Construction
The child:

- introduces terminology to assist more complex classification, e.g.
  These numbers are even. I'll add them to this group.
- extends descriptions to include a range of words for each item, e.g. large, heavy, rectangular
- includes definitions and generalisations, e.g.
  All of these animals are warm-blooded so they should have backbones.

Responsiveness of Child as Speaker
The child:

- incorporates descriptive language when completing classification tasks
- elaborates on, or justifies, groupings
- effectively describes attributes and functions of items
- attempts to make generalisations based on less obvious characteristics, e.g.
  I know birds can fly but an emu doesn't fit the group. I'll need to think of another grouping.
- offers evidence to substantiate classification, e.g. *They all breathe under water*

EXPANDING

The child completes classification tasks efficiently, using groups or subgroups. Self monitoring and adjustment are evident.

Text Content and Organisation
The child:

- includes elaborated descriptions of items
- provides cohesive and comprehensive response to classification activities
- consistently shows an understanding between attributes, functions and classification categories

Vocabulary and Sentence Construction
The child:

- uses terminology and detailed descriptions to support classification decisions
- links generalisations and evaluations to produce a comprehensive set of classification criteria
- uses subject specific vocabulary to describe classification decisions

Responsiveness of Child as Speaker
The child:

- independently classifies and substantiates choices
- responds to questions with elaborated detail or justifications
- demonstrates logical links between items and classification decisions
- incorporates abstract classification choices
- uses a wide range of vocabulary during classification activities e.g. *Oxygen is in the water*

CLASSIFICATION

Indicators

BEGINNING

Responsiveness of Child as Listener
The child:

- shows minimal response to the task
- responds to literal questions with one-word answers, e.g.
  Red. Long. Black.
- asks questions to complete grouping activities, e.g.
  Here? Like that?

DEVELOPING

Responsiveness of Child as Listener
The child:

- responds to comments made, e.g.
  Yes, they're big. I think they go there.
- responds to questions with more detail and justification for groupings
- requires teacher support to extend discussions

CONSOLIDATING

Responsiveness of Child as Listener
The child:

- responds with evaluative comments, e.g.
  I could have put them here.
  I think that's the best place.
- responds to questions about concrete or abstract groupings
- asks questions to clarify information provided

EXPANDING

Responsiveness of Child as Listener
The child:

- responds confidently and effectively to comments or questions
- answers to questions demonstrate an ability to make concrete or abstract classifications
- asks a wide range of questions to clarify information or substantiate groupings

Chapter 4:

Supporting Diversity Through Oral Language

The *Oral Language: Developmental Continuum* has been written as a way of helping teachers to 'map' children's progress and make decisions about teaching practice on the basis of their observations, within a 'whole language' approach to learning. However, not all children will necessarily follow the same 'map' and there may be differences within individual development and across groups of learners, particularly in relation to children for whom English is not a first language. Their progress will be determined by previous experience and the context in which learning takes place. Thus, within the 'First Steps' framework, it is most important to take account of cultural, linguistic and religious background.

In addition to this it is important to recognise that many children, for whom English is not a first language, come to school with a vast range of knowledge and competence in other languages. Often, these children are learning to use more than one language. Consequently they are making complex choices about the appropriate type and form of language to use in particular contexts. Thus, for many children language would seem to be one of their most powerful assets, one which needs to be built upon and extended, if they are to realise their full potential.

Finally, when planning ways of helping children to become more effective communicators, we need to consider what we are helping children to do with language and how this is being done. If we want children to become more powerful communicators of their ideas and to be able to reflect critically on the ideas of others, then this has implications for helping children to become autonomous learners in the classroom context. In order to build on cultural and linguistic diversity in a way that allows children to have more control over their learning, there are a number of issues which need to be considered. They will be explored under the 5 areas presented in the following model:

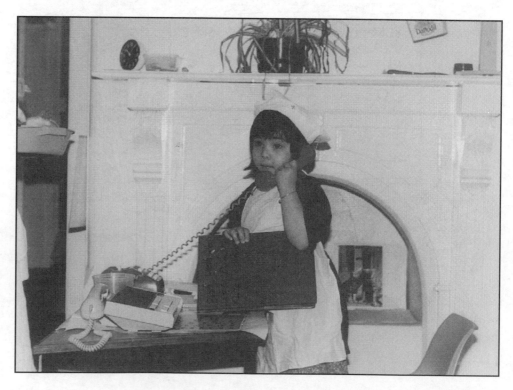

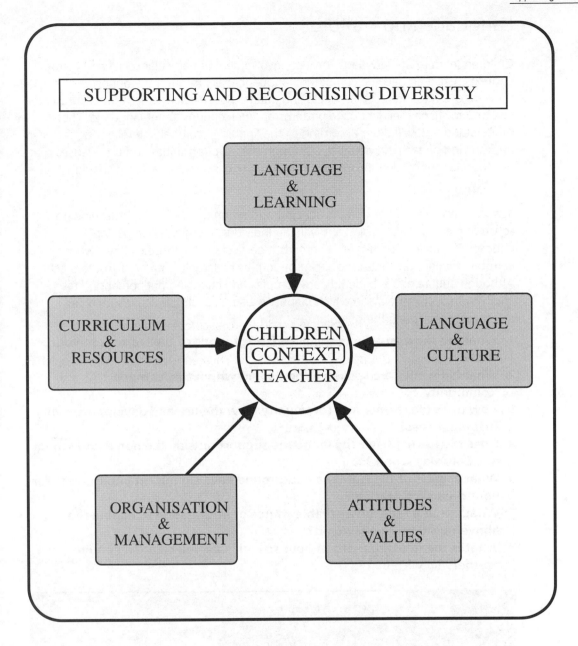

SUPPORTING AND RECOGNISING DIVERSITY

LANGUAGE & LEARNING

CURRICULUM & RESOURCES

CHILDREN CONTEXT TEACHER

LANGUAGE & CULTURE

ORGANISATION & MANAGEMENT

ATTITUDES & VALUES

NB. Children who do not speak English as their first language come to school with varying levels of linguistic competence, ranging from one language to several. It is very hard to describe this particular group of children, with any degree of accuracy, in a way that captures the complexity of their developing skills. This group includes children who are bi-dialectic as well as bilingual and multilingual. Because the term 'non-English' sometimes implies a deficit model of language, the term 'bilingual' will be used to identify children for whom English is not a first language. Although this term is also fraught with difficulty, it seeks to recognise that many children are developing English in addition to one or more languages.

Language and Culture

Children learn to use language through involvement in particular social and cultural contexts. Children become competent language users through the opportunities they are given to interact with peers and adults. The social activities that children are involved in shape their language patterns and perceptions about language. These 'understandings' will differ according to the linguistic, cultural and religious background of each individual. It is through these opportunities and experiences that the foundations of identity are laid. Thus language is a major factor in shaping identity.

School plays an important part in shaping and affirming the learner's developing sense of identity. Recognising and valuing individual identity has important educational implications for all children but particularly for those children whose cultural, religious and linguistic background may be largely unfamiliar to the teacher. Although culture and self identity are complex and changing phenomenon, it is important to look at ways in which identity is being constructed and supported in the community and in the school:

1 **What are the cultural and religious backgrounds of the learners in your class?**
2 **What languages are spoken at home and within the learner's 'community'?**
3 **How does the learner and community view the use and development of first languages?**
4 **Does the learner have any language support outside the home and school e.g. Saturday school?**
5 **What aspects of the learner's background have significant implications for your classroom practice?**
6 **What might be the most reliable source of information to enable the above questions to answered?**
7 **What is the role of parents in your school? Can you create a genuine partnership with parents?**

Attitudes and Values

Attitudes come from the teacher, the children, parents/caregiver and the community at large, and permeate and influence classroom life in both overt and hidden ways.

Attitudes are reflected through:

a interaction with children and adults in the school context;
b the curriculum and associated resources;
c the organisation and management of learning.

All classrooms manifest values of one kind or another. The question is whose value system is embodied in your classroom, and what are the consequences of this for the children in your class and the community at large?

Because attitudes and values are so deeply embedded within us, they are difficult to identify and perhaps even more difficult to modify or change. However it might be useful to start exploring the way in which your attitudes are reflected in your interactions with the children in your class.

1 **Are you aware of the range of different cultural interactional styles in your classroom? This includes culturally based action and beliefs such as :**
   • **body movements**
   • **gestures**
   • **holding-hands**
   • **eye contact**
   • **lip movements**
   • **interpretation and use of silence**
   • **forms of address**
   • **appropriate use of left and right hands**
   • **interaction with and responses to adults**
   • **learning styles and beliefs about how to learn**
   • **beliefs about gender and age appropriate behaviour.**

195

2 **Are you aware of the values and cultural norms that are reflected through the learner's language? For example:**
  • **In some Asian languages humility, deference and respect to elders are reflected in speech;**
  • **Speech acts, e.g. politeness, are also culturally bound;**
  • **Tone, stress and intonation are also important indicators of meaning which vary across languages.**

3 **Do you appear to value and respond to some children's contributions more than others? Why is this?**

4 **Consider your expectations of individual or groups of children. What are these based on?**

5 **What is your attitude to the recognition of diversity and difference? How is this reflected in your practice?**

6 **Are the learners in your class able to share and explore experiences and understandings that are important to them, which may be unfamiliar to you?**

7 **How do you respond to incidents that are perceived as racist, by you, the children or the parents?**

8 **Do you take account of the wishes and expectations of parents? How do you respond to these?**

9 **Given the discrimination and hostility that is experienced by some communities, how do you address this in your teaching?**

Organisation and Management

The learner's developing sense of self, understanding of others and appreciation of diversity and difference can be greatly enhanced by the way in which the classroom is organised and managed. Although interactions are highly complex and many decisions are made on a moment to moment basis, it can be very revealing to 'step back' and consider particular aspects of classroom practice.

It may be useful to explore the following practices:

1 **How you group children. Do you encourage children from different ethnic groups to work together and share their cultural and linguistic backgrounds? Do you encourage children from the same linguistic background to work together so that they can explore concepts in their own language?**
2 **How you take individual needs into account, particularly in relation to cultural and religious practices, e.g. appropriate clothing and changing arrangements for sport, particular dietary requirements etc.**
3 **How you give responsibility, reward and sanction children and on what basis you make these decisions.**
4 **How you assess children. Do you take cultural and linguistic factors into account when evaluating children's progress?**

Curriculum and Resources

The content of the curriculum and how it is taught embodies particular views about language and learning and about what is valued. Resources and materials convey messages which have a powerful influence on the learner's developing understanding of the world and their place in it. Resources that reflect the diversity of Australian culture clearly give a different message to resources which tend to convey only one aspect of Australian society.

1 **When considering resources it is useful to identify who is represented, how they are represented and what they are doing. Do the resources represent cultural diversity? Do the resources reflect the achievements and contributions of a range of people from different cultural backgrounds?**
2 **How can you help children to read texts critically, eg. to identify bias, stereotyping, omission, accuracy and challenge the 'authority' of the text?**
3 **What is the place of equal opportunity in curriculum planning? Does the curriculum maintain inequalities or identify and confront them?**
4 **Does the curriculum reflect individual differences within the classroom as well as the diversity of Australian society as a whole?**

Language and Learning

Community Languages

The maintenance and development of the learner's community language(s) within the classroom is a controversial and complex issue. However, if as suggested earlier, language is seen as central to the learners developing a sense of self and intellectual growth, then support for community languages is fundamental to learning.

As well as providing a link between home and school, research suggests that emerging competence in one language can actively support the development of a second language, while enabling the learner to master new concepts.

In addition to this, recognition of community languages gives important messages to children who are not bilingual as well as enriching the language climate of the classroom. Finally, the support that children get influences not only their own linguistic development but the language use of their communities.

Even if you do not share the community languages of your children, there are a number of ways in which support can be given.

1 **How are community languages recognised and valued throughout the school?**
2 **Are children encouraged to use their community language in the classroom? Are they encouraged to talk, read and write in their own languages?**
3 **Do the children's skills in their community languages form part of your assessment procedures?**
4 **Are monolingual children encouraged to develop an understanding and use of languages other than English?**
5 **How many school staff share the community language of the children?**

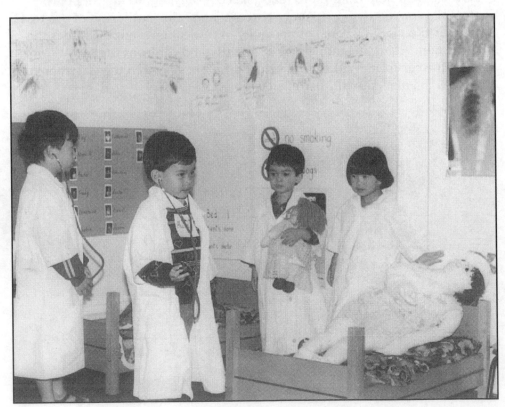

English as a Second Language

There are many ways in which English as a second language can be developed in the classroom context. Decisions about the 'best' way rest with the teacher's knowledge of the children and the context in which the teaching and learning is taking place. However it is possible to consider the relationship between what the learner brings to the classroom and factors that may influence the development of English.

1 To a greater or lesser extent the learner already 'knows' about how their first language works in particular contexts for specific purposes. Thus the learner brings a wealth of knowledge and experience into the classroom which forms the basis of their understanding and further development.
   On the whole this 'transfer' is extremely positive and many surface 'errors' are recognised as developmental, but there may be some aspects which are problematic and need particular attention. These are related to:
   • pronunciation
   • stress, rhythm and intonation
   • grammatical structure.

2 Although culture is constantly evolving, it is possible to identify culturally specific interaction styles which may differ radically from that of the teacher. Knowledge of these differences has important implications for effective classroom practice, e.g. in some cultures students do not question what the teacher says; in another culture this may depend on whether the teacher is male or female.

3 Children in the early stages of becoming bilingual may need time to tune-in to the sounds, rhythm and intonation patterns of English. At first some children may wish to watch and listen, or join in, but not contribute verbally in English. For young children, this may be an especially distressing time. To be in an unfamiliar situation , where no-one seems to understand what you are trying to say may be a very frightening experience. Hence the need to find ways of supporting the learner's community language while creating opportunities to hear and use English.

4 Much research suggests that, as with first language development, second language development is facilitated through interaction, i.e. children learn a second language by using it. In the classroom context, language and learning are seen as inextricably linked and development is thought to take place through the child's readiness to make meaning from the context. If this view is accepted, it is possible to identify key features within a classroom context that will support second language development.

199

Key Features of Support for English as a Second Language

Planning activities in which children need to talk

This gives the learner a reason to communicate. Activities that are culturally relevant and appropriate and match the learner's intellectual level ensure cognitive and linguistic involvement. Providing an environment in which learners feel confident to use English and are willing to take risks is central to development, e.g. dramatic activities, barrier games, retelling stories, problem-solving activities, excursions, interactive games, Chinese Whispers, presenting cultural viewpoints etc.

Planning activities that are practical

In the early stages of development, if meaning is embedded in the 'here and now', learners are able to relate actions and objects to words and phrases. As far as possible, learning should be based on active participation in a range of different activities involving practical problem solving, exploring and creating through the use of multi-media, e.g. board games, card games, speaking at assembly, morning talks, introducing visitors, role play acceptable behaviour, discussing and negotiating classroom rules, how to…demonstrations, telephone conversations, making videos/radio shows, taped interviews with staff and other students etc.

Planning activities in which learners need to collaborate

Through collaboration children build on each others' talk, extend their range of phrases and negotiate meaning. This enables the learner to play an active part in the activity and contribute at their own level, e.g. make a story—each person is given a piece of a story and with their group they need to decide where their part of the story fits into the story sequence, matching cards—children must listen to and ask questions of other children in a group to ascertain who has the card/s they require, provide an at work table, special days, making group models, find your partner, word games etc.

Planning activities in which the process leads to the repetition of particular language

This is especially helpful in the early stages of development. Repetition gives the learner the opportunity to take part in the activity and practice and consolidate specific language in meaningful contexts. Making specific reference to particular vocabulary and phrases at the beginning of an activity helps clarify meaning, e.g. jigsaw words, exchanging information (likes and dislikes), teaching something to another child, deliver messages to other children/teachers/administration staff, activities which establish correct speaking and listening courtesies, oral retell of stories/story maps, turn taking games etc.

Planning for time to talk

It is very useful to build in time for learners to talk about the activity after they have completed it, as well as during it. This demands particular language skills and enables the teacher to help the learner extend their use of English and consider the next series of activities. Feedback helps the learner reflect on their language and learning and take an active part in planning for further development, e.g. teacher or student planned reflection in pairs; small groups, self-evaluation to peers of activity/learning carried out, sharing individual work with teacher, parent or another student, activity maths, circle sharing, recounting experiences, describing and explaining, swapping stories and jokes, speaking and listening corner etc.

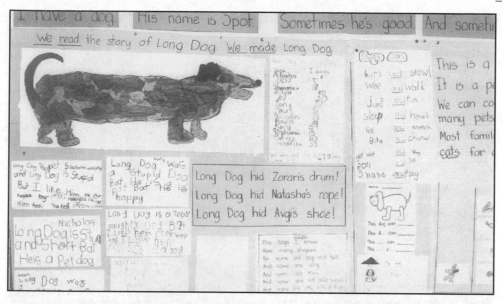

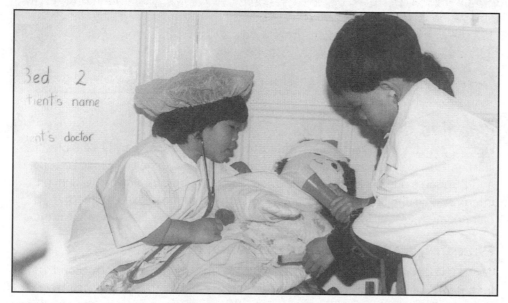

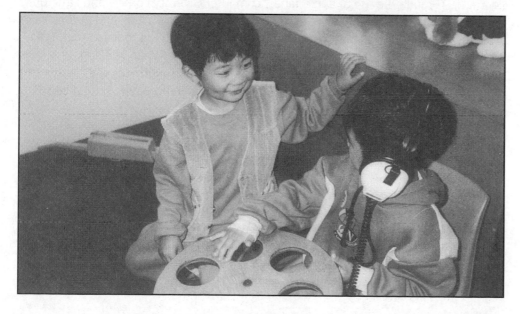

Planning for continuity

Exploring a particular theme or concept through a number of activities enables the learner to consolidate and extend particular types of language in a range of contexts and through a number of different curriculum areas. Projects allow individual interpretation and independent learning within a shared context, e.g. teacher planned activities for modelling particular communication skills—taking turns etc.

Planning a supportive environment

The classroom environment can provide another means of supporting second language development, if it is designed to enable children to manage their own learning. Through the use of audio tapes, computers, literacy corners and structured play areas, to name but a few, learners can work at their own level and at their own pace. It is important that print is strategically placed around the room so that it may be accessed easily i.e. place print at an appropriate height. When working on a particular theme, for example—Birds—place any books brought into the classroom around the Birds display so the children can locate the books easily.

Planning for diversity

Part of becoming fluent in a second language involves recognition of the cultural conventions that are embedded in that language. Learners need opportunities to explore the differences between English and their home languages and consider the way in which these conventions influence interaction in different contexts.

Planning ways of assessing development

This should include the learner's use of English and their first language in a range of contexts and take account of code switching as part of their developing sophistication as language users.

The Teacher's Use of English

In addition to the above features, the teacher's use of English has a significant impact on the learner's development of English as a second language. Judging what is appropriate and when, should be based on knowledge of the children's level of understanding and individual needs. Although this is not easy, observation and profiling can help identification.

Being systematic

In the early stages of development it is important to enable learners to hear and use particular phrases, in a range of contexts, from a number of sources. Very often children will 'pick-up' particular phrases and use them as a means of 'getting started' and 'joining-in' other children's talk. Monitoring your own use of language becomes central to enabling the learner to use and make sense of the new language. The balance between using particular phrases 'consciously' and sounding 'natural' is a delicate one. Supportive strategies include:

- Identifying, and where appropriate, modifying language to be used in specific activities;
- Being consistent;
- Using repetition;
- Checking for understanding.

Being supportive

There are a number of ways in which teachers can encourage children to use English, while at the same time providing models for the learner to try out. Giving the learner time to contribute, encouraging repetition, prompting, rephrasing and praising are some of the strategies that appear to be facilitative. With older children it may be possible to talk about specific aspects of English and make comparisons between English and the learner's home language. Learners can be encouraged to use particular strategies to help development such as asking for clarification, translation, etc.

Being continuous

As the learner becomes more fluent in English it is important to continue to give support. Particularly in relation to curriculum areas, where some terms and vocabulary are specific to the subject. Cummins (1984), suggests that it takes up to 3 years for young children to become fluent in conversational skills but it may take up to 7 years for children to acquire 'academic' language.

Being aware of possible difficulties

In order to help the learner to become fluent it is important to identify areas which may cause the learner some difficulty, in relation to structure, pronunciation and intonation. Listening to the language choices children make to construct meaning as well as listening to the message, enables the teacher to identify difficulties as well as development. Some difficulties may need specific attention to ensure they do not become permanent.

Being sensitive

Finally, however fluent children become in their second language, if this is at the expense of their community language, their loss will be greater than their gain. Thus it is important to support simultaneous development within a context which values and promotes diversity, while fighting discrimination.

Caroline Barratt-Pugh
Anna Sinclair

Appendix 1 - Question Topic Cards (see page 152)

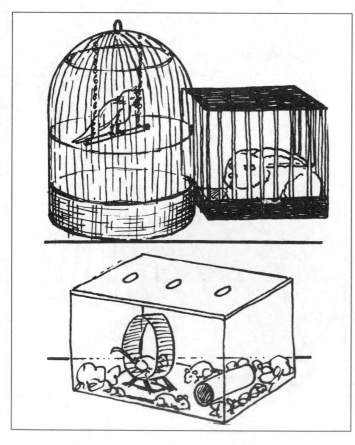

Appendix 2 - Twenty Questions Game (see page 163)

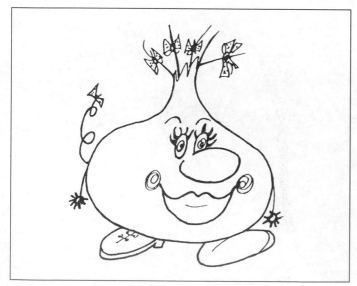

Appendix 3 - Character Role plays (see pages 89–93)

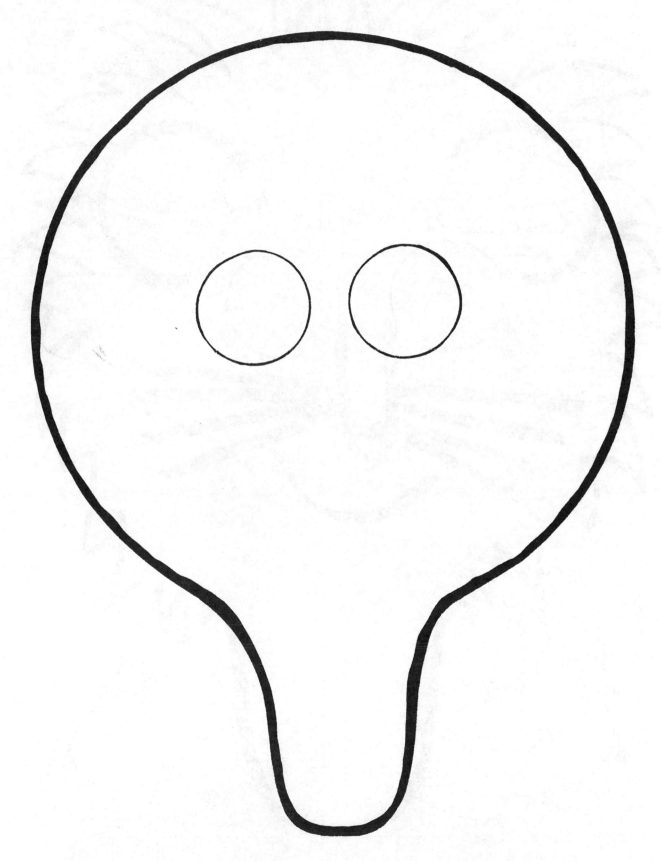

209

211

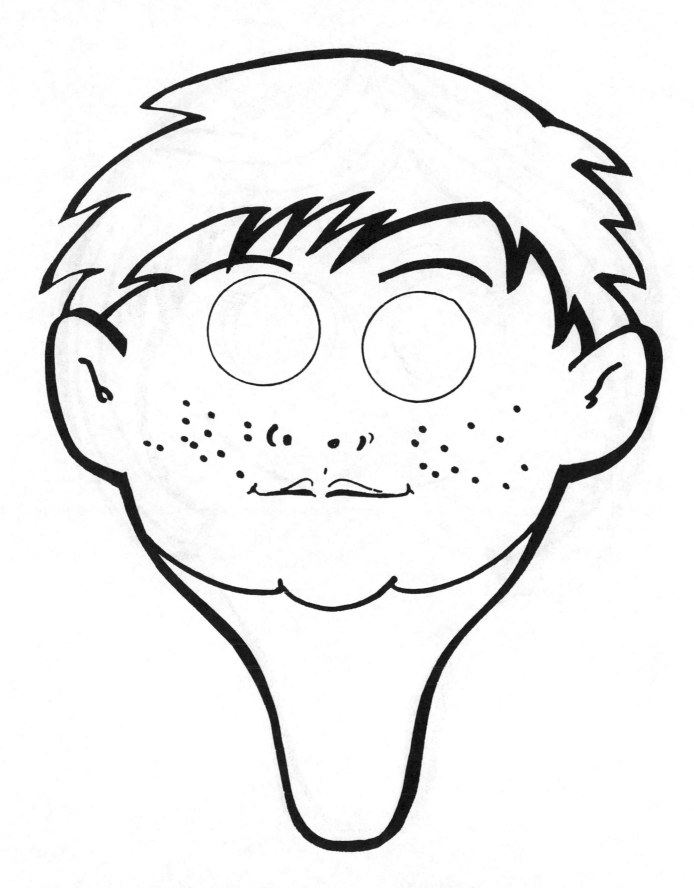

Published by Rigby Heinemann

215

Appendix 4 - Story Reconstruction (see pages 94–7)

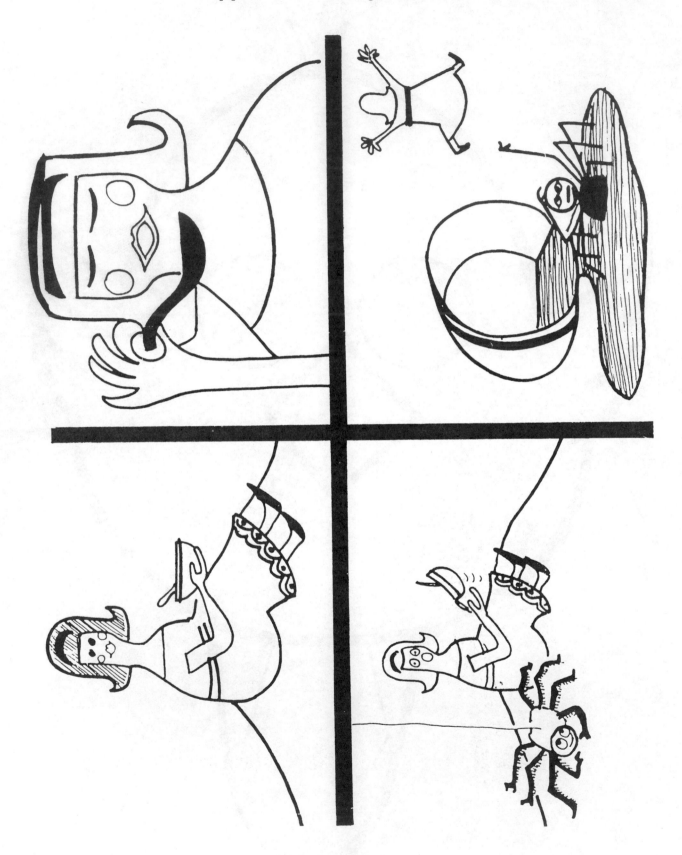

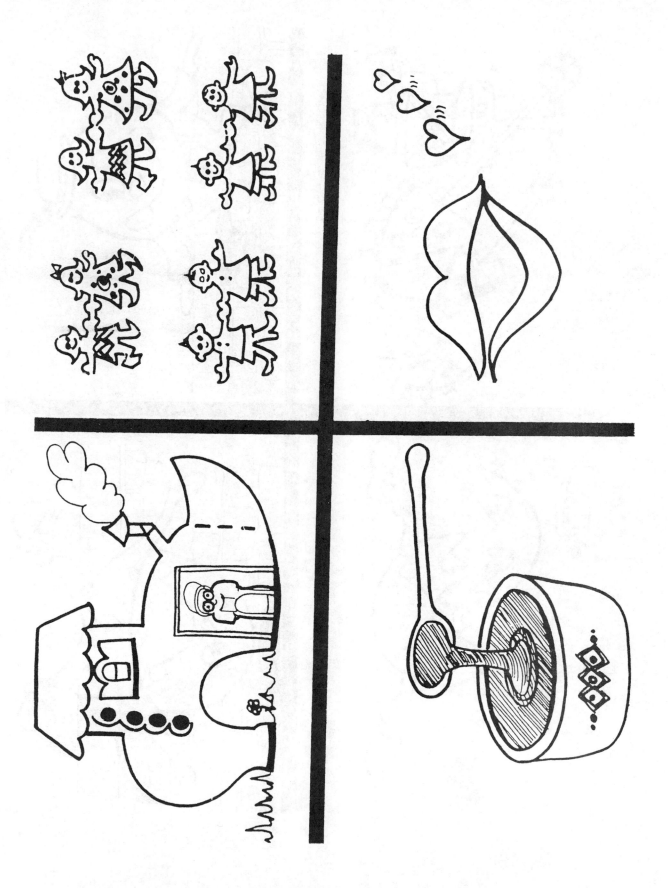

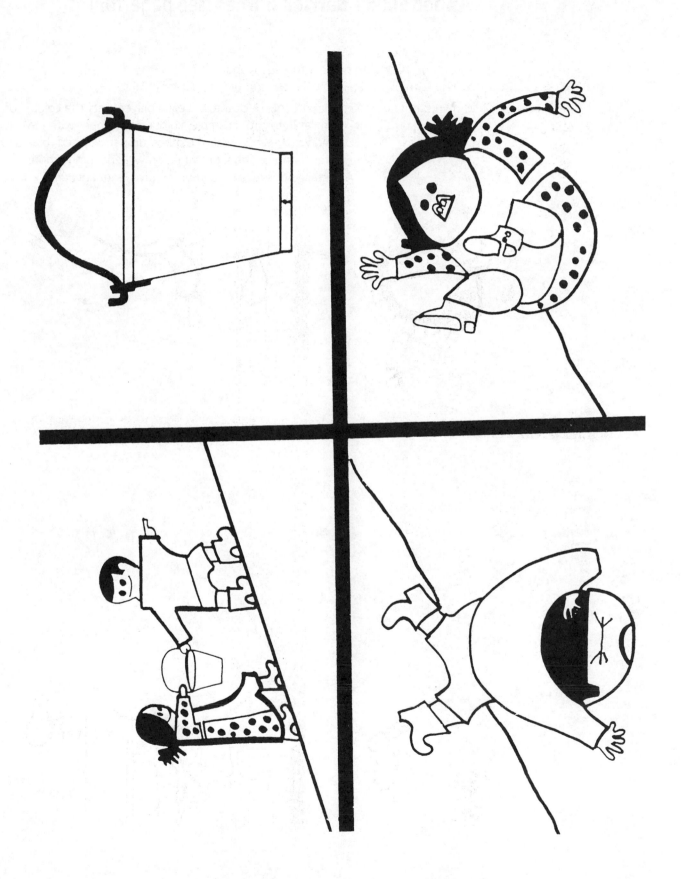

Appendix 5 - Barrier Games (see page 109)

- Make 2 sets for each game.
- Expand sheets to A3 size.
- Colour, back with cardboard and laminate.
- Use with plastic animals, people, cutouts or counters.

Clown Barrier Game – Make 2 sets of clothes for each player. Vary the colours of similar items; for example, colour one jumper with red, blue and yellow stripes and the other jumper with red, blue and green stripes. The slight variation will encourage more detailed observation and descriptive language.

223

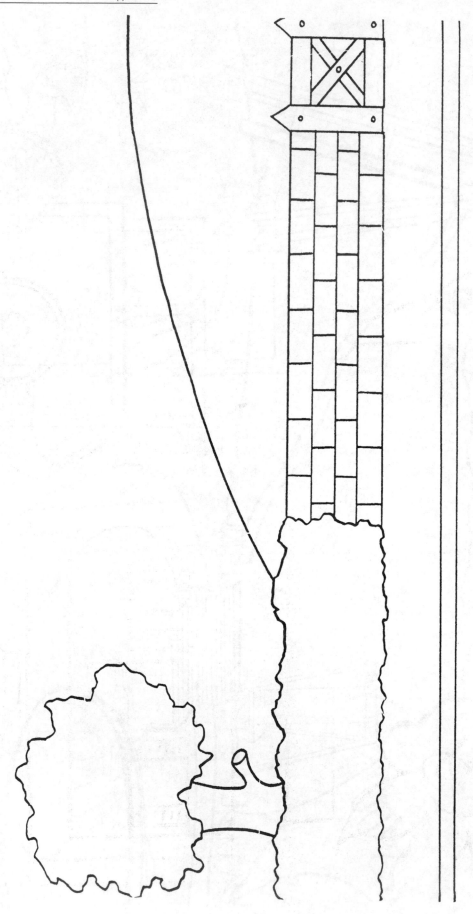

 Published by Rigby Heinemann

225

227

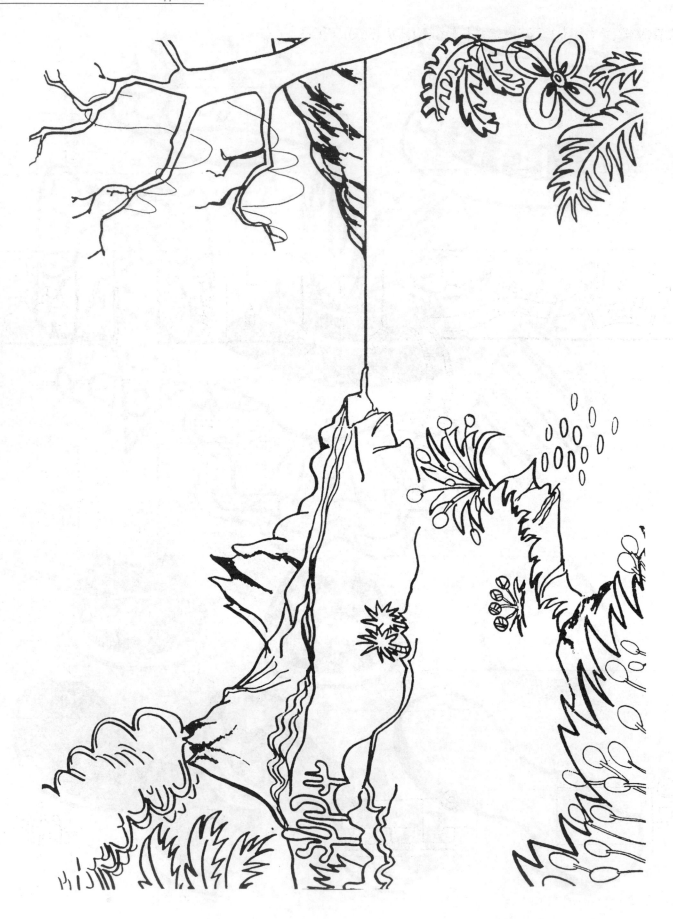

Appendix 6 - Crossroads Activity (see page 127)

231

Acknowledgements

The Gosnells Oral Language Project was initiated in 1989 by Principals and K–3 staff in the following schools:

Ashburton Drive Primary School
Gosnells Primary School
Huntingdale Primary School
Seaforth Primary School
Wirrabirra Primary School and Education Support Centre

The First Steps Project acknowledges the contribution made by staff members in producing a valuable oral language resource that has been implemented in many schools throughout Western Australia. Teachers and support staff involved in the Project were:

Coordinators
L. Allen (Project Content)   J. Smailes (Project Organisation)

Key Teachers
P. Deubert   C. Gorey   A. Hey   B. Malins   R. Milligan
J. Naylor   N. Patroni   S. Smith   J. Turner

Principals
J. Burton   A. Choules   P. Peckham   J. Glendinning   K. Green
W. West   G. Templeman

Project Consultant   Dr B. Shortland-Jones

Special thanks to the following teachers for their assistance in developing and trialling the instructional strategies:

C. Stone   S. Paterson   R. Talbot   S. Brown   D. Mathieson
C. Murphy   P. Deubert   A. Roberts   L. Gardiner   N. Patroni
K. Jerrat   L. Patterson   S. Allen   A. Kane   W. Tillman

The Newstelling section was written by Jean Rice and Leanne Allen for the *First Steps Project*. Appreciation is expressed to the following people:

(i)   Staff at the Carlisle Language Development Centre during 1986–87. The key role of Marilyn Hand in this initial development is especially acknowledged.

(ii)   Fourth-year students in 1986 and 1987 from the Department of Speech and Hearing Science (Curtin University of Technology).

The First Steps Project is also grateful to Caroline Barratt-Pugh and Anna Sinclair for their valuable contribution in preparing Chapter 4: Supporting Diversity Through Oral Language and to Kay Kovalevs for her dedication and hard work in the editing and co-ordination of the First Steps books in the early years of the project.

Further Reading

Applebee, A. N. 1978, *The Child's Concept of Story,* University of Chicago Press, Chicago.

Brice-Heath, S. 1983, *Ways with Words: Language, Life and Work in Communities and Classrooms,* Cambridge University Press, Cambridge.

Brice-Heath, S. 1986, What no bedtime story means: Narrative skills at home and school, *Language in Society*, 59-76.

Cummins, J. 1984, *Bilingualism and Special Education, Issues in Assessment and Pedagogy*, Multilingual Matters, Clevedon Avon.

Hammon 1990, Is learning to read and write the same as learning to speak? in *Literacy for a Changing World*, ed. J. Christie.

Lahey, M. 1988, *Language Disorders and Language Development,* Macmillan, New York.

Perera, K. 1984, *Children's writing and reading: Analysing classroom language*, Basil Blackwell, London.

Rothery, J. 1984, The development of genres - primary to junior secondary school. in *Language Studies: Children Writing, Study Guide,* ed. Deakin University Press.

Sloan, P. and Latham, R. 1981, *Teaching Reading is…*, Thomas Nelson, Australia.

Tizard and Hughes 1984, *Young children learning: Talking and thinking at home and school*, Fontana, London.

Wells, C. G. 1986, *The Meaning Makers: Children Learning Language and Using Language to Learn,* Heinemann, Portsmouth, New Hampshire.

Wells, C.G. 1987, The language experience of five year-old children at home and school, in *Literacy, language and schooling*, ed J. Cook-Gumperz, Heinemann, Exeter, New Hampshire.

Westby, C.E. 1985, Learning to talk—talking to learn: Oral-literate language Differences, in *Communication skills and classroom success: Therapy methodologies for language-learning disabled students*, ed. C.S. Simon, Taylor and Francis, London.

Westby, C. 1986, Learning to talk, talking to learn, in: C. Simon, *Communication Skills and Classroom Success: Therapy Methodology for Language Learning Disabled Studies*, College Hill Press, San Diego, California.